MAPS & SKETCHES
FROM GEORGIAN & EARLY VICTORIAN
BIRMINGHAM

PLAN OF BIRMINGHAM - 1805

Five Ways

Hagley Row

Islington Row

Birmingham Canal

To Dudley

Turnpike

Summer Hill Street

Camden Street

PARADE

Giles & Forrest's Brewery

Warstone Lane

Great Hampton Street

To Soho

Bath Row

Brass Works

Wharf

Wharf

Crescent

Worcester Canal

Holloway Head

Wharf

Hospital Street

Bristol St.

Bromsgrove Street

SummerLane

Hospital

B

E

D

Bath Parsonage

I

Walmer Lane

Barford Street

River Rea

13

15

Britannia Brewery

To Lichfield

Wharf

Steam Mills

Hicks's Square

Union Mill

Bradford Street

Warwicks Street

Bordesley

Mill Lane

Floodgates

Coopers Mill

Warwick's Canal

Wharf

Prospect Row

Ashted Row

Canal to Fazeley

Barracks

18

Drawn by
Js. SHERRIFF
of Oldswinford
late of the Crescent
BIRMINGHAM.

River Rea

Vauxhall

REFERENCE
A St. Martin's Church.
B St. Philip's Church.
C St. Barthol's Chapel.
D St. Mary's Chapel.
E St. Paul's Chapel.
F St. John's Chapel.
G New - Meeting.
H Old - Meeting.
I Free School.
J Theatre.
K Charity School.
L Moat House.
M Quakers Meeting.

REFERENCE
1 The Square
2 Colmore Row
3 Temple Row
4 Edmund St.
5 St. Paul's Square
6 Caroline St.
7 Church Street
8 Congreve St.
9 Paradise St.
10 Hill Street
11 Horse Fair
12 Smalbrook St.
13 Bull Ring
14 Moseley Street
15 Aulcester St.
16 Bordesley Street
17 Bartholomew St.
18 Great F...ke... St.
19 Temple... Street

MAPS & SKETCHES FROM GEORGIAN & EARLY VICTORIAN BIRMINGHAM

PAUL LESLIE LINE
ADRIAN BAGGETT

FOREWORD BY WILLIAM DARGUE
POEMS BY IAN HENERY

MAPSEEKER ARCHIVE PUBLISHING

Published by Mapseeker Archive Publishing Ltd, Mapseeker Studio, 30 High Street, Aldridge, Walsall, WS9 8LZ, Tel: +44 (0)1922 288111 / +44 (0)1922 458288

Printed by Wyndeham Grange Ltd, Butts Road, Southwick, West Sussex, BN42 4EJ, 01273 592244

British Library Cataloguing in Publication Data.
A catalogue record for this book is available from the British Library.

ISBN 978-1-84491-816-4 Softcover
ISBN 978-1-84491-819-5 Hardcover

Typesetting and origination by Adrian Baggett

Historical maps available to buy at
www.mapseeker.co.uk

CONTENTS

I can't find Brummagem
Composed by James Dobbs – sung by him in 1828 on the
stage of the Theatre Royal – New Street Birmingham

I can't find Brummagem
Full twenty years, and more, are past
Since I left Brummagem,
But I set out for home at last,
To good old Brummagem.
But every place is altered so,
There's hardly a single place I know;
And it fills my heart with grief and woe,
For I can't find Brummagem.

As I walked down our street,
As used to be in Brummagem,
I know'd nobody I did meet;
They change their faces in Brummagem.
Poor old Spiceal Street's half gone,
And the poor old Church stands all alone,
And poor old I stand here to groan,
For I can't find Brummagem.

But 'mongst the changes we have got,
In good old Brummagem,
They've made a market of the Mott [moat]
To sell the pigs in Brummagem.
But what has brought us most ill luck,
They've filled up poor old Pudding Brook,
Where in the muck I've often stuck
Catching jackbanils [sticklebacks] near Brummagem.

But what's more melancholy still
For poor old Brummagem,
They've taken away all Newhall-hill,
Poor old Brummagem!
At Easter time, girls fair and brown,
Used to come roly-poly down,
And show'd their legs to half the town,
Oh! the good old sights of Brummagem.

Down Peck Lane I walked alone
To find out Brummagem,
There was a dungil [dungeon] down and gone!
What no rogues in Brummagem?
They've taken it to the street called Moor,
A sign that rogues they get no fewer,
The rogues won't like to go there I'm sure,
While Peck Lane's in Brummagem.

I remember one John Growse,
A buckle-maker in Brummagem;
He built himself a country house
To be out of the smoke of Brummagem;
But though John's country house stands still,
The town itself has walked up hill.
Now he lives beside a smoky mill
In the middle of the streets of Brummagem.

Amongst the changes that abound
In good old Brummagem,
May trade and happiness be found
In good old Brummagem;
And though no Newhall-hill we've got,
Nor Pudding Brook, nor any Mott,
May we always have enough to boil the pot
In good old Brummagem.

FOREWORD
BY WILLIAM DARGUE

Birmingham has always been energetic in destroying and rebuilding itself, and in this city of constant change Birmingham folk have often taken pride in the new developments while at the same time bemoaning the disappearance of their old buildings.

In 1828 Birmingham comedian James Dobbs stood on the stage of the Theatre Royal in New Street and sang his own composition, 'I can't find Brummagem'.

True to form, Dobbs would no longer be able to find the Theatre Royal! In 1961 it was replaced by the Woolworth Building, a block which stands on New Street opposite Bennetts Hill. With the Woolworth's store also gone, James Dobbs would now be singing his plaintive ditty in the kitchen of the Bella Italia restaurant.

Dobbs goes on to lament the loss of his childhood haunts and the fact that he recognises no-one in the streets, the town being largely filled with newcomers. In one verse he points out a feature that became a theme of the town's development. He notes that the country house built well away from the industrial centre by wealthy buckle-maker John Growse, now stands next to a smoky mill. The town had overtaken Growse's rural retreat as it spread relentlessly outwards, the erstwhile well-to-do districts being turned over to industry in a remarkably short time.

Although a prosperous market town from the 12th to the 16th century, Birmingham had remained relatively small and compact, its population of some 5000 matching those of present-day Coleshill or Studley, though much more densely packed than either.

THEATRE ROYAL IN NEW STREET 1829

However, with its central place in the Industrial Revolution, Georgian Birmingham saw a massive and rapid expansion of industry especially in the iron trades and in 'toy' making, the manufacture of small items of high quality. Encouraged by improvements in the national road network and by the cutting of the canals, trade and the town grew rapidly, attracting entrepreneurs, craftsmen and working people from across the Midlands and beyond. Within a hundred years the population grew fivefold to some 31,000 inhabitants and by 1770 Birmingham was the third most populous town in Britain after London and Bristol.

There was an enormous expansion of building within the town and around its rural edges. Existing timber-framed houses in the centre were given neo-classical brick facades or more frequently were demolished and rebuilt in brick, many with three storeys instead of two as previously. A good number of public buildings were erected, all of which were designed in neo-classical styles: churches and religious meeting houses, a library, post office, schools and the Theatre Royal.

Writing in 1783 Birmingham's first historian William Hutton, a native of Derby, recalled his first sight of the town. He was impressed:

> Upon Handsworth Heath, I had a view of Birmingham. St. Philip's Church appeared first, uncrowded with houses, untarnished with smoke, and illuminated with a Western sun. It appeared in all the pride of modern architecture. I was charmed with its beauty, and thought it the credit of the place . . . . the buildings in the exterior of Birmingham rose in a style of elegance.

However, Hutton was less impressed with the buildings that housed the majority of the population, maintaining that quantity had given way to quality: 'The stile of architecture in the inferior sort, is rather showy than lasting.'

During the following hundred years the population continued to boom, increasing by over sixteen times to nearly half a million inhabitants in 1871. And the frenetic building activity continued unabated, the town expanding ever outwards as the remaining spaces in the densely packed centre were filled and older buildings made way for new.

There was amongst many observers unrestrained excitement and enthusiasm for this rapid change and progress. However, the main focus of the guide books of the time was not the architecture of the town, but the impact of industry and the incredible diversity and ingenuity of technological advance. James Drake in 1839 was struck by Birmingham's *'dense cloud of smoke issuing from its confused mass of buildings, and brooding over it in sullen gloom',* because it represented for him the victory of man over the natural world, the casting of iron, the variety of innovative processes and the resultant ingenious products. (James Drake 1839 Road Book of the London & Birmingham and Grand Junction Railways) It is at this time that the celebrated Birmingham epithets were coined: *'the first manufacturing town in the world', 'the City of a Thousand Trades', 'the Workshop of the World'.*

There was pride too in the development of the buildings of the town, piecemeal and unplanned though this was. The timber-framed houses crowding the market area round St Martin's church were cleared and handsome new buildings erected along the High Street and Bull Street most with shops on the ground floor. Cut in the 12th century and one of Birmingham's oldest streets, New Street was by 1830 again new and considered the best street in the town with its many shops, public buildings and important establishments, a street along which to promenade. Around the junction with Colmore Row the demolition of *'mean and straggling erections'* was commended and their replacement with 'a variety of ornamental buildings' was lauded. One of these was the Town Hall; others were the handsome stuccoed buildings on Bennetts Hill and Waterloo Street, some of which still stand. (Beilby Knott & Beilby 1830 Sketch of Birmingham)

However, by the middle of the 19th century there were already those who realised that change was occurring so quickly that all vestiges of old Birmingham would soon be gone with no record of their ever having existed. Later in the century it was commonplace for intellectuals and increasingly the general public to want to preserve old buildings: the Society for the Protection of Ancient Buildings was founded in 1877, the National Trust in 1884.

However, in Birmingham Thomas Underwood was an early pioneer in his appreciation of the disappearing past. Around the middle of the century he began a project to find and publish (1866) visual records of the town's old and demolished buildings and to record those still standing. It was the memory of the *'mean and straggling erections'* that he wanted to keep.

An artist and lithographer, Underwood was not involved in saving the buildings themselves, but in preserving their memory. Unusually, he was especially interested in the ordinary buildings of the town. He recognised that there already existed drawings of the town's public buildings. The first history of Birmingham by William Hutton had plates showing Birmingham churches, the General Hospital and the Market Hall, *et al.* And subsequent guides to Birmingham showed similar scenes. But Underwood was keen to make available images of less prestigious buildings, some of which had been demolished within his lifetime, others whose future was uncertain. The majority of these were the run-of-the-mill buildings that would never appear in any guide book: pubs, forges, shops and houses, many dating from the 18th century, some from as early as the Tudor period.

It is as well that Underwood published when he did. While the destruction and redevelopment of much of the Victorian city centre during the 1960s is well-known, remembered and now lamented, the almost total replacement of 16th-, 17th- and 18th-century Birmingham during the second half of the 19th century is less known. True, there were many buildings which were no longer fit for purpose and many were even unfit for habitation, but it is sobering to think, as you look at Underwood's fascinating collection, that of all the buildings shown, the only ones still standing are the timber-framed Old Crown in Deritend and The Golden Lion (now in Cannon Hill Park), St Philips' Church (now the Cathedral) and St Martin's-in-the-Bull Ring (of which only the tower remains from Underwood's time).

Birmingham changed almost beyond recognition during Underwood's own lifetime; he died aged 73 in 1882. But thanks to his personal project to make a visual record of the town, we now have available to us an invaluable record of a vanished Birmingham.

William Dargue 2013

THE OLD CROWN

THE GOLDEN LION

ST PHILIPS' CHURCH

ST MARTIN'S-IN-THE-BULL RING

ACKNOWLEDGEMENTS

This book is a culmination of many long hours of passionate and meticulous work by those who were enthused by the idea of its creation. I would like to express my grateful thanks and acknowledgments to everyone who has played a part, and of course the gift from the two outstanding men of the 19th century, who have made it possible to reflect on the many buildings now long since gone, and that we can now share with our children and friends how old Birmingham looked two centuries ago.

William Dargue, one of Birmingham's accomplished historians for his splendid introduction and Ian Henery, Walsall Poet Laureate, for his captivating poems that enrich the visual resources.

A special thank you to Adrian Baggett for his illustrative skills and visual representation of the many resources utilised. Steve Toulouse and Phil Bradney for their many hours of meticulous and painstaking work digitally transforming the rare original volumes along with the antique town plans for the book. John and Julie Swann for supporting the editorial work and research

Berian Williams and Steve Bartrick for their sourcing of additional antique views and vistas used in the book and Lynn Hughes for her wonderful pencil and charcoal drawing of the "Stagecoaches".

Paul Leslie Line 2013

W. WADDELL, HEN & CHICKENS HOTEL, NEW STREET.

INTRODUCTION

The last two known remaining volumes of "The Building's of Birmingham Past and Present", the first published in 1866 and the second published in 1869 were this year purchased from a London rare books dealer and have now been safely brought back to Birmingham, secured wholly intact for prosperity. Last year when I first became aware of these wonderful sketches that had been made by the well known Thomas Underwood, it was sad to see the remains of one volume, (1866) being stripped down so that the plates could be sold on the antique prints market. It seems ironic that the very reason the volumes were created in the first place was at the request of many at that time who had long desired that the sketches taken of many of Birmingham's less important buildings, even earlier in that century should not remain in private hands, but they should be accessible to the many who like to describe to their children or their friends how old Birmingham looked many years before.

Samuel Timmins, writing under the pseudonym of "Este", notes in the introductory essay from 1866, in the first volume, that "the public buildings are always sure to be frequently sketched and published … but the ordinary street architecture is considered too common-place to be preserved in any form; and a century or two hence it will be impossible to recall what sort of places our modern towns now are".

Indeed he was accurate in his predictions; many of the buildings captured in sketch form by the celebrated Thomas Underwood featured in the original volumes disappeared when the railway companies extended their railways to the heart of the town during the 1840's. Buildings in the unsavoury "Froggary" district, a network of courts and alleys, were demolished. Entire streets such as Peck Lane, Colmore Street and King Street disappeared, at the same time one of the most frequented public houses, the Hen and Chickens on New Street was torn down. Many more buildings disappeared later in the 19th century following Joseph Chamberlain's "Improvement Scheme" that saw many new streets being cut with rows of Victorian Building's replacing many of the older Georgian buildings. More than a century on from that change "modern day" glass faced skyscrapers tower over what would be a totally alien and unrecognisable Birmingham to both Thomas Underwood and Samuel Timmins.

This publication includes all of the original sketches from both volumes of "The Buildings of Birmingham Past and Present", digitally re-mastered and art worked. The descriptive, poignant and captivating poems especially created for this publication by Ian Henery, poet laureate for Walsall, add a rich and sometimes nostalgic dimension. In addition there are rare maps such as the recently acquired Survey of the Birmingham Canal Navigations 1864 and period town plans that feature many of the buildings captured in sketch, and a collection of elegant and fascinating manufacturing trade plates, ensuring that the original request – all those years ago, is fulfilled for our future.

Paul Leslie Line 2013

THE BUILDINGS OF BIRMINGHAM

PAST AND PRESENT

VOLUME ONE 1866

WHILE the poet can find "sermons in stones" and "books in the running brooks," the intelligent observer can always trace the chief features in the history of a town by the nature of its buildings and the development of its streets. Just as the old Roman towns and the cathedral cities and medieval places generally have their characteristics so clearly marked in the arrangement of their streets, the quiet of their "Close," or the quaint picturesqueness of their remains, so even our most modern towns preach "sermons" in their "stones," their "stucco," or their" brick," and reveal the history of their origin and growth. The experienced eye of the archeologist can determine with singular accuracy the date of a building and the history of a district, just as a comparative anatomist, like Cuvier or Owen, can restore an extinct being from fossil or osseous remains. As every generation has its tastes, its fashions, its foibles, and its aspirations shown in every detail of its life, so these are developed and made most permanent when they are exhibited in the buildings of a town. The old half-timbered houses of three centuries ago have been followed by the Elizabethan mansions, the Jacobean halls, the Anne and Georgian houses, the Regency stucco, and the modern variegated brick in Gothic style. The existence of any one of these styles will always indicate within a very few years the history of a town. The fashion of the day is generally followed in the decoration of the person and in the building of a house. Very few are bold enough to follow a very ancient fashion, or to anticipate what the good taste of the next generation may approve. Hence all buildings, as well as all other fashions, are more or less distinctive, more or less characteristic of the times in which they were produced.

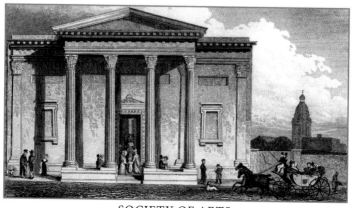

SOCIETY OF ARTS

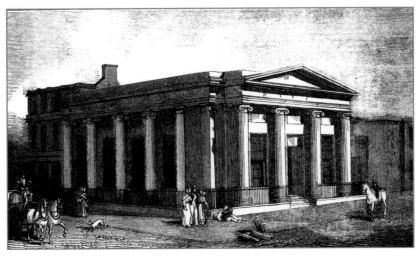

THE NEWS ROOM

The history of Birmingham may be seen by an intelligent stranger, no matter by what road he enters our streets. If he arrives by the old Warwick Road, he soon discovers that he is in the oldest part of our town. He finds in the Old Crown House and the quaint old houses opposite, examples of some of the oldest buildings which Birmingham can boast He traces many other less marked remains as he proceeds, and finds examples of the Anne and Georgian era, right and left, as he advances towards St Martin's Church, and in that church he sees what the taste of a century ago and the tests of our own time have done. If he comes through Handsworth he finds marked traces of the rapid growth of our town at the beginning of the 1800's: and if he comes through Edgbaston he sees the wonderful increase of wealth marked by the handsome suburban houses which have been built during the past twenty years since writing this volume.

The public buildings are always sure to be frequently sketched and published for general circulation, as the most prominent and important features of every town: but the ordinary street architecture is considered too commonplace to be preserved in any form; and a century or two hence it will be impossible to recall what sort of places our modern towns now are. Only in such very rare cases as those of Pompeii and Herculaneum are all the features of a town preserved *in situ* for the future, and hence the deep curiosity and intense interest which are excited by those buried cities of the olden time. Such as the placards and hand-bills of our time will scarcely survive a century, except in the cabinets of the curious, so the aspect of our streets is changing so completely that, in a very few years, very few examples of our existing buildings will remain; and hence the interest and value of the sketches which this volume contains, as examples of the present and relics of the past.

Although less remarkable than many large towns for the antiquity, variety, and number of its old buildings, Birmingham has many which are interesting in many ways; and as the march of improvement is continually removing or changing the appearance of these relics of old days, it has been thought desirable to publish these sketches

THE OLD WORKHOUSE

of what Birmingham was and is. Happily the love of the past, the conservative element of the English character, is very fairly developed, even in our democratic town. The affectionate regard with which all old Birmingham people look on the old streets and buildings of the town; and the regret which all feel when an ancient landmark is removed or an old feature is defaced, are among the most healthy and hopeful signs of our time. Fortunately for those of us who belong to the present generation, such men as the late David Cox, Samuel Lines, J. V. Barber, Thomas Underwood, and others took the trouble to sketch the buildings of Birmingham as they existed from thirty to sixty years ago, and have thus preserved many characteristics of our town, now long ago removed. Those Warwickshire Drawings—interesting not only from the names of the artists, but from their local value—will be held a century hence in high honour as records of what our town and county were while the nineteenth century was young.

The present volume is issued at the request of many who have long desired that the sketches taken years since should not remain in private hands, but that they should be accessible to the many who like to describe to their children or their friends how old Birmingham looked half a century ago. They are not intended to be exhaustive or complete; but they will, it is hoped, excite considerable interest, and lead to the preservation and publication of other memorials of the history of our town. It has not been thought necessary to increase the size and the cost of this volume by pictures of public buildings which have been often drawn, engraved, and published in so many forms, but to limit these sketches to those which represent buildings removed during the last half century, or threatened during the next few years. If our local rulers were half as careful about the interests of posterity as they are where financial matters are concerned, they would make it imperative that a sketch and plan of every old house should be deposited in the Borough archives before that house could be pulled down.

The Illustrations in this volume are mostly

VIEW FROM THE TOP OF NEW STREET 1829

original and published for the first time; and if some of them represent buildings and streets comparatively insignificant, it must be remembered that these were once important parts of our town, and that no other record of them has been preserved. The "fashionable quarter" of one generation becomes the "slums" of the next, and the "degrading" process proceeds so rapidly that it is interesting to watch what changes it has produced even in our own time. The houses in Edgbaston Street, for example, which were inhabited around 1785 by some of the principal inhabitants of our town, have long been deserted and left to become manufactures, warehouses, or shops. The well-to-do houses around St. Bartholomew's and St. Mary's have undergone great changes as to tenancy; and the front gardens before the Broad Street houses are rapidly being covered with shops. The New Street Station has removed off the face of the earth, a mass of old houses which were some of the best in Birmingham in the mid 1700's, and of which not a trace now remains.

The nature and extent of this Introduction will not allow any definite description of the growth of Birmingham, or a comparison of its condition at various times, and the materials for such a review may be readily found elsewhere. As, however, the larger part of these Illustrations relate to the Birmingham of the latter half of the 18th century, it may be advisable to give a short extract relating to that era. This passage is quoted from that almost unworked mine of the materials of history of our town during the last century, *Aris's Birmingham Gazette*, and is curious as giving a local designation long since disused :—

"From an accurate survey made at Midsummer last (1786), it was found that there were 173 streets, 9770 houses (6032 front and 3738 back), exclusive of Deritend and that part of the town called the Foreign; and by computation the number of the inhabitants are 53,735."

The object of this work being to give the Illustrations rather than to describe them, it will be necessary to add only such few details as maybe readily accessible, since the materials for a full description and history of the various buildings cannot be collected and arranged without years of labour and research. Many of the places represented are not known to have any special or important history, and only their outward form is sketched. In many cases, probably, if the memories of some of our oldest inhabitants were questioned, many curious matters of local interest and tradition might be recovered; and it is hoped that some into whose hands this volume may fall will take the trouble to set down what they may happen to know concerning the origin, history, and fate of many of the old houses pictured in this work. An annotated copy of this volume, with such memoranda so many now living could easily contribute, would form one of the most valuable local legacies which could be bequeathed.

Samuel Timmins 1866

EARLY 19TH CENTURY VIEW ACROSS BIRMINGHAM

"THE PLAN OF BIRMINGHAM, SURVEYED IN 1731,

Is one of the most valuable of the few materials which exist from which an adequate conception can be formed of the growth, the progress, and the changes of our town. A full examination of this curious map, and a comparison of it with those of later years, will be found to be most interesting and instructive. The general arrangements of the streets remain pretty much the same now as then; but several of the names have been changed. St Martin's Parsonage, with its moat and picturesque garden, and the larger moat where Smithfield now stands, has all been removed. The many plots of garden ground, the Cherry Orchard and the Bowling Green, the Welch Cross* and the Old Cross have long since disappeared, and we can scarcely realise the fact that they existed almost within our own time. St. Martin's Parsonage, however, occupying the angle between Pershore Street and Smallbrook Street, remained as late as

1825, when the land had increased in value—nearly £10,000, as compared with £5,556 nineteen years previously in 1806. This remarkable map shows also the Cold Bath and the "Lady Well," now despised and doomed, but once famous for the good water it supplied; the "Steel Houses," from which Steelhouse Lane takes its name, and the other less-known "Steel House," in Coleshill Street; the "Corn Cheaping," now the Bull Ring; the "High Town and Beast Market," now High Street; the "Broad Street," now Dale End; the " Mercer or Spicer Street," now Spiceal Street; the houses all round St. Martin's Church; a large extent of gardens and orchards where some of our busiest streets now stand and our densest population is hived. How clear, and pleasant, and smokeless the Birmingham of that day was one brief extract may show:-

"On Sunday last, December 31, 1739, a rose in full bloom, and several fine rose buds, were plucked in an open garden belonging to Mr. John Green, of New Street in this town, which is esteemed a very extraordinary circumstance at this advanced season of the year"

*Later spelt as Welsh Cross

Drawn by David Cox.

Engraved by W.Radclyffe.

ST MARTIN'S PARSONAGE

Where is Birmingham
(Inspired by "I Can't Find Brummagem" by James Dobbs)
Poem by Ian Henery

I have come home to the town of my past
But there's hardly a single place I know
Haunts of my youth have gone and I feel woe,
My heart in tatters and I feel downcast.
How has Birmingham been altered so fast?
The streets are the same and not re-arranged,
It's just that so many names have been changed,
I always thought my Birmingham would last.

St Martin's Parsonage, garden and moat,
Removed and the moat where Smithfield now stands
Demolished, destroyed, by a butcher's hand.
Plots of gardens gone, who on earth can gloat
Eden's loss, home or blackbird and whitethroat?
The cherry orchard and the bowling green,
Welch Cross and Old Cross, places loved and seen,
Long disappeared, their memory I dote.

These sites existed within our own time,
St Martin's Parsonage on Pershore Street,
A spiritual oasis, a heart beat,
All gone – but what was the terrible crime?
A picturesque garden, beauty sublime,
Pulled down by town planners with hearts of stone,
A great haven they could not leave alone
My epitaph, my sad lament, in rhyme.

All gone – the Cold Bath and the Lady Well,
Famous for the good water it supplied,
Now despised and doomed, pollutants, its died:
We have turned our garden into a Hell.
Gone the nightingales in their sylvan dells,
The "Steel Houses" in the old Steelhouse Lane,
Once shattered husks with broken window panes,
Birmingham bewitched and under a spell

WELCH CROSS
FORMERLY STANDING IN DALE END, NEAR TO BULL ST.
TAKEN DOWN MARCH 1803

Gone, too, the less known "Steel House" in Coleshill
And the old Corn Cheaping, now the Bull Ring;
A marvel where you could buy anything:
Fresh bread, shoes or woollen clothing from the mills.
Happy days to linger and eat your fill
Obliterated, they have been pulled down
Deemed unworthy of our Birmingham town,
Gone, but their memory comforts me still

The Beast Market now the High Street today,
Mercer Street is Spiceal Street and Dale End
Was Broad street, it is hard to comprehend
The oasis of orchards could not stay.
Cut down for profit, higher rents to pay,
But were under streets where people are hived.
Please tell me – what is left? What has survived,
A smokeless Birmingham that's gone away?

OLD CROSS
FORMERLY STANDING IN THE BULL RING ON THE
SITE NOW OCCUPIED BY NELSONS STATUE
TAKEN DOWN AUGUST 1784.

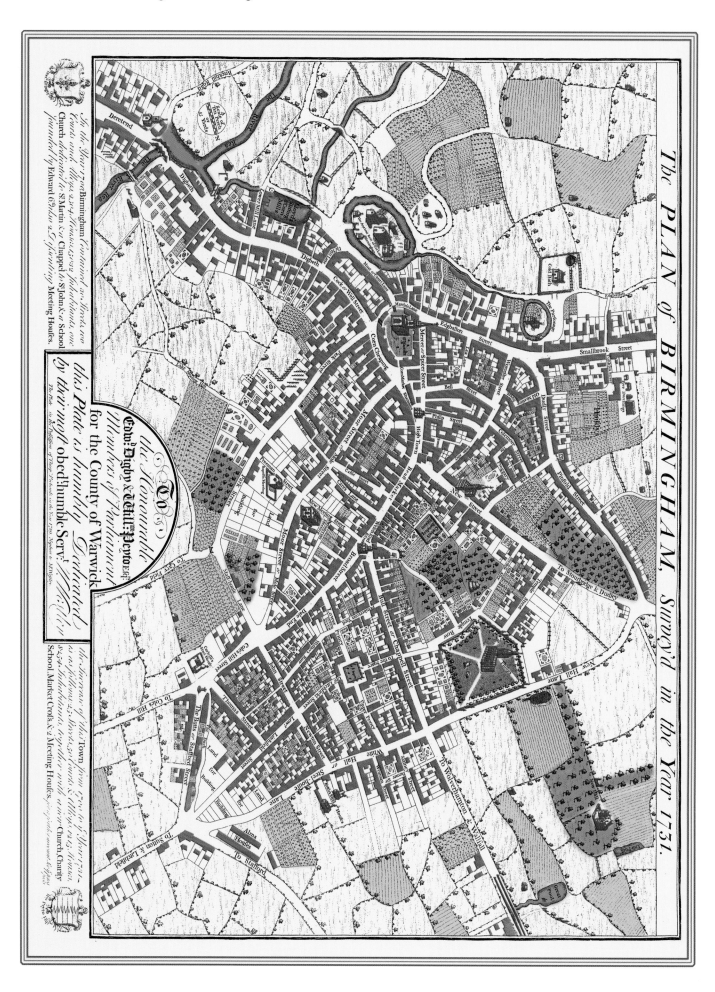

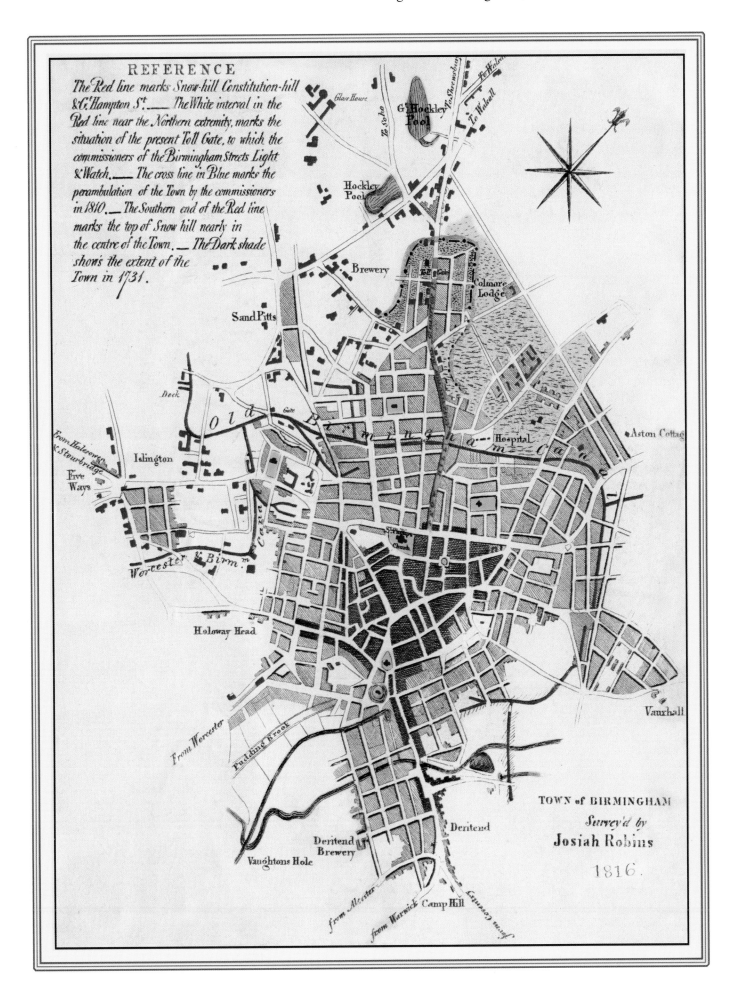

"BIRMINGHAM MEN OF THE LAST CENTURY"

The plate showing the Birmingham men of the last century may very appropriately follow the Map of the town in which many of them were born, or became famous in local annals more than a century ago. The letter-press description gives nearly all the details now known, and it will be seen that several of them were able and distinguished men, of whom every lover of Birmingham would gladly know more. Birmingham has been much maligned, as an unintellectual town; but the residence of each men, engaged in ordinary business pursuits—the fact that several libraries flourished, and the Old and New Libraries were founded—and that about the same period our town had its Lunar Society, with such men as Boulton, Watt, Priestly, Darwin, Galton, and Murdock among its residents and neighbours, will place Birmingham on a level with almost any other place of its size and age. The proposed formation of a Library of Foreign Books, and the following Prospectus, which appeared in 1785, are no mean indication of the intellectual activity of our town eighty years ago:—

"Birmingham, June 6th, 1785 .—It is proposed to publish, some Original Essays, in the manner of the Spectator, by a Set of Gentlemen of this town, and its neighbourhood. "The first Number (which is intended as a Specimen) will be printed on Saturday next, Price two-pence and those Persons who are desirious to encourage the Undertaking, are respectfully informed, that the Printers hereof will receive any Letters or Papers calculated for this Work which is designed for general advantage, and will be entitled The Tutor."

BIRMINGHAM MEN OF THE LAST CENTURY

In presenting the above Key to the purchasers of Eckstein's well-known Tontine Painting of "BIRMINGHAM MEN OF THE LAST CENTURY," it has been thought desirable to append thereto a very brief biographical notice of each personage, for the purpose of reviving and sustaining the once eminent interest which for a considerable length of time deservedly attached itself to these celebrities, who were highly esteemed and applauded by a very large number of their fellow citizens and countrymen for the political opinions peculiar to their body, and which were strongly opposed to the views advocated by the numerous and wealthy Tory party of the day.

When it is taken into consideration that the nightly debates and the clever productions of these worthies gave birth to and assisted in diffusing those great and glorious principles which in after years resulted in the passing of the Reform Bill, the Catholic Emancipation Bill, together with other progressive measures, and mainly contributed towards infusing into the hearts of "the people" those sentiments of liberalism and loyalty which experience has proved to have been productive of highly beneficial effects—taking these and similar facts into consideration, the Print may almost be looked upon as possessing a national as well as local interest, and hence it became more than desirable to supply the following biographical sketches for the information of such as would otherwise be unacquainted with the avocations and peculiarities of the several characters represented.

No. 1.—MR. JAMES MURRAY, a Linen and Woollen Draper. Mr. Murray resided in Moor Street, was a Member of the Antiquarian Society of Scotland, and was most generally known by the name or title of "Cheap John." He emigrated to America, to which place his two sons and two daughters soon afterwards followed him.

No. 2.—MR. JOHN WILKES, a Cheese Factor, corner of Carr's Lane and High Street, and subsequently held a commission as Captain in the Militia.

No. 3.—MR. JOHN FREETH, or *Poet* Freeth, as he was almost universally styled, kept a Tavern at the corner of Lease Lane and Bell Street, at whose house this Social and Convivial Party nightly met. They were nicknamed the "*Jacobin Club*" and the "*Twelve Apostles*," in consequence of which, at a Tavern in Peck Lane, kept by Joe Lindon, over the fire-place in the room in which the opposite or Tory Party were in the habit of assembling, was printed in large clear type, "*No Jacobin admitted here.*" In the preface to an edition of his Songs and Poems Mr. Freeth writes "My hobby-horse and practice for thirty years past has been to write songs upon the occurrence of remarkable events; and nature having supplied me with a voice somewhat suitable to my style of composition, to sing them also, while their subjects were fresh upon every man's mind; and, being a Publican, this faculty, or rather *knack*, of singing my own songs, has been profitable to me; it has in an evening crowded my house with customers, and led me to friendships which I might not otherwise have experienced." Many of Mr. Freeth's published poetic effusions possess the merit and sterling animus peculiar to Dibdin's popular songs, whose style they closely resemble. He died September 29th, 1808, in the 78th year of his age, leaving behind him two sons and eight daughters. Upon his tombstone, in the Old Meeting House Yard, are the following appropriate lines:

"Free and easy through life his wish to proceed,
Good men he revered, be whatever their creed;
His pride was a sociable evening to spend,
For no man loved better his pipe and his friend."

No. 4.—MR. RICHARD WEBSTER, Brass Founder, Moor Street, left no issue.

No. 5.—MR. JEREMIA VAUX, Surgeon, Moor Street, Medical Officer to the Associated Militia of the period, held a very high position in the town as a professional man, being both clever and experienced. He was a most inveterate snuff taker.

No. 6.—MR. JOHN COLLARD, Hatter and Tailor, High Street, was very fond of discussion, and a most able Logician, upon which latter subject, retiring to a pretty sylvan cottage, near the Bell and Cuckoo, he wrote and published his "Essentials of Logic," "Praxis of Logic," and other elaborate treatises. A mezzotint portrait of Mr. Collard was published in the year 1808, from a picture by Lonsdale.

No. 7.—MR. JOHN MILES, Edgbaston Street, Patent Lamp Manufacturer, whose business was subsequently carried on by Mr. Blakeway.

No. 8.—MR. SAMUEL TOY, Newhall Street, Steel Toy Manufacturer, was a man possessing very buoyant spirits and an inexhaustible fund of wit, humour, and satire. In after life he was reduced in circumstances, and became landlord of the Mitre Inn, where he died after a very brief illness, although he boasted, a short time before his death, of not remembering having ever been under the hands of a medical man.

No. 9.—MR. JAMES BISSET, kept a Bazaar and Museum, in New Street, and being the longest liver of the twelve, he ultimately became possessor of the Tontine Picture. Late in life he removed to Leamington, where he continued to keep a Museum until his decease. One evening, whilst living in New Street, and suffering most acutely from an attack of gout, two of the Club, agreeably to a pre-concerted plan, entered his sitting room disguised as highwaymen and well armed, roughly demanded his money, and, as was expected, Mr. Bisset resisted, and, forgetting his gout, actually chased the supposed robbers to Freeth's house in Bell Street, where the practical joke became at once apparent, and, strange to say, he never again suffered from the same excruciating complaint, to which he had for a long time previously been a martyr. Another anecdote has been related to the writer of these sketches by an eye-witness, which afforded a "striking exhibition" of the bitterness of party feeling, which ran high at the period referred to (Circa 1790). One evening Mr. Bisset had the temerity to call in at Lindon's, the Tory house, in Peck Lane, when one of the company indecently puffed a volume of smoke into his face. Up to this moment Mr. Bisset had submitted with perfect indifference to the many petty annoyances and insulting observations made indirectly *at* him, but the moment an indignity was directly offered *to* him, he resented the insult by felling the offender to the ground. A general mêlée took place, which ended in Bisset's summary ejection into the street, and a breakage of glasses and jugs, &c., amounting to nearly five pounds, which Mr. Bisset had to pay, being sued for the amount in the Court of Requests. He was considered a connoisseur of paintings and works of art. The following is a copy of the inscription on the tombstone erected to his memory by his friends and admirers, in the church yard at Leamington:—

SACRED TO THE MEMORY OF
JAMES BISSET,
Who died August 17, 1832, Aged 72 years.
This Monument was erected by his Friends in token of their respect
to his memory.
DOROTHY BISSET,
Died December 14th, 1825, Aged 62.

No. 10.—MR. JOSEPH FEARON, Tin Merchant, Digbeth, was constable of the town for many years, and considered the leading speaker of the Jacobin Club, being a most fluent and clever orator. Eckstein has represented Mr. Fearon in the act of addressing his confreres. He was known by the sobriquet of "Lord North," from his advocacy of that statesman's principles and conduct in connection with the American war. His constant theme, whenever possible to introduce the subject, was his favourite idea of appealing to appointed Committees of Arbitration in lieu of the expensive and uncertain process of law suits, an opinion which was very determinedly maintained by the late Silk Buckingham, Esq. Mr. Fearon left one son.

No. 11.—MR. JAMES SKETCHLY, Moor Street, Auctioneer, Appraiser, and Valuer. He was, by several years, the senior member of the Club.

No. 12.—MR. JOSEPH BLUNT, Brazier, High Street. He left two sons.

THE FOLLOWING M.S. MEMORANDUM IS ATTACHED AT THE BACK OF THE PAINTING.
"This picture is the common property of the twelve following gentlemen represented on the reverse, to be disposed of at all times as a majority of them shall think proper, and to be the sole property of the survivor.

"JAMES SKETCHLY,	"JAMES MURRAY,	"JOSEPH FEARON,	"JOHN COLLARD,
"JOHN FREETH,	"JOSEPH BLUNT,	"JEREMIA VAUX,	"JAMES BISSET,
"JOHN MILES,	"RICHARD WEBSTER,	"SAMUEL TOY,	"JOHN WILKES."

The Picture painted by John Eckstein, 1792.

Thomas Underwood, Lithographer and Printer, Castle Street, Birmingham.

Birmingham Men of the Last Century
(painting by John Eckstein, 1792)
Poem by Ian Henery

My name is John Freeth, write poems, sing songs,
I run a busy Birmingham tavern;
It's here that the 12 Apostles belong,
To argue and sing songs in our cavern.
Twelve of us to benefit the nation,
Debating through the night at our leisure
Any topic of consideration:
The Reform Bill and progressive measures.

My name is James Murray or just "Cheap John"
And I used to sell antiques in Scotland;
I live in Moor Street, two daughters, two sons,
I now sell woollen clothing in England.
I like Birmingham but its not for me,
I'm off to America, the New World:
There's riches to be made across the sea,
The new United States flag is unfurled.

My name is John Wilkes, a lover of cheese,
I've a cheese factory in the High Street;
When I'm with the Apostles, I'm at ease,
John Freeth's a tavern is a great place to meet.
We hold our regular nightly debates,
Birmingham thinks we are slightly esteemed,
Controversial topics we will berate,
Whilst ordinary mortals are in dreams.

My name is Richard Webster, I'm in brass,
A factory in Moor Street of renown;
Too busy for children, I'm upper class,
I'm the new gentry of Birmingham town.
The 12 Apostles gather and we sup,
History may not remember our names
Or John Freeth's poetry, deep in our cups,
Our lives hot wax beneath the candle's flame.

My name is Jeremia Vaux, surgeon,
I'm a man you don't want to meet every day;
I'm clever and an important person,
Lowly beginnings, I've come a long way.
The Apostles, we sing to each other,
Celebrating libraries that have flourished:
We pioneers, we Birmingham Brothers
And that our children are not malnourished.

My name is John Collard, a logician,
I publish philosophical treatises;
"Praxis of Logic", I love discussion
Whilst other men (like John Wilkes) love their cheese.
In our town new libraries are being founded
And that's worth carousing with all my friends;
Essentials of logic keep me grounded,
Nights with the Apostles I like to spend.

My name is John Miles, I come here to think;
I live in Edgbaston Street and make lamps.
The 12 Apostles, we debate and drink,
It gets me out of lodgings that are damp
And a camaraderie that is sustaining
Against the Judas Kiss of betrayal.
Human life on earth, our clocks are waning,
Enacted in this painting's portrayal.

My name is Samuel Toy – I make Toys!
I live in Newhall Street and like a laugh
Filling John Freeth's tavern with fun and joy,
Good on the humour but bad on the maths,
Business suffered so bought the Mitre Inn.
We 12 Apostles, in this last meal
Remember Judas, betrayal and sin,
The last Supper and friendship that is real.

My name is James Bisset, martyr to gout,
A museum in New Street and a bazaar,
A pugilist, I will stand in a bout,
I'm a fighter's fighting man, a real star.
Words and fists with rivals and highwaymen,
You must sometimes fight for what you believe;
The Apostles, our like not seen again,
Birmingham, our last supper, weep and grieve.

My name is Joseph Fearson from Digbeth,
The 10th Apostle, I'm a constable,
The Apostle Spokesman before my death.
The leader, the one responsible,
Evidenced as a lawyer for Birmingham.
Honary titles, I'm in the tin trade
But enforce order against all bedlam,
Only then can Birmingham's wealth be made.

My name is James Sketchy, an auctioneer
From Moor Street, I'm Apostle 11;
Betrayal is what humans deeply fear,
Did Judas ever go to heaven?
Judas a traitor, but its really time,
Betrayal in the sealing of a kiss,
A measured life-span considered a crime,
Betrayal is time, much on earth to miss.

My name is Joseph Blunt, I'm into coal,
The High Street, of the Apostles, the last,
A message in this painting for your soul.
Birmingham, hear our warning from the past:
Time is the Judas, the great betrayal,
A poet's kiss and you will hear our words,
The last Supper, our final portrayal,
A historian's kiss and we are heard.

"THE OLD CROWN, DERITEND,"

Is a copy of a drawing, made about forty years ago, of the oldest and most interesting building of our town. The picturesque aspect of this old building, and the facts relating to its history, make it one of the famous houses of old time. Fortunately, it is the property of a gentleman who guards it with jealous care, and has spared no cost or trouble to preserve a building which is one of the ornaments and honours of our town. The "deeds" alone, relating to this ancient house, being continuous and complete for four hundred and fifty years, are highly interesting; and the story of this "faire Mansion house of timber," which Leland saw as he rode through the "pretty suburb into Birmingham town," has been so fully given in Mr. Toulmin Smith's most valuable work that no further details need be given here. Few men have the learning or the leisure to produce so important a work as "The Old Crown House," but if every owner of such ancient buildings would communicate what he knows to those who are specially interested in such matters, a most valuable mass of local history would soon be acquired.

OLD CROWN, DERITEND - c1825

"THE GOLDEN LION."

Nearly opposite The Old Crown is another remarkable example of those half-timbered gabled houses which made old streets so marvelously picturesque. Although less remarkable than the fine old house just named, the Golden Lion is a good specimen of the old houses in Deritend when Rupert displayed his "burning love for Birmingham" three centuries ago, and destroyed several similar houses which existed at that time. The Golden Lion and the house on each side have no special story, and the deeds which relate to the property disclose no very important facts. Closely connected, however, with Deritend history is the highly interesting series of facts discovered by Mr. Toulmin Smith respecting the foundation of the Chapel of St. John, proving it to be one of the earliest results of Wiclif's teaching, and the independent spirit of the "men of Birmingham" of the olden time. As the Chapel is in no way picturesque and has been sketched before, we may pass it, and turn for a moment to two pictures showing what sort of a place the Deritend district was, with the remark that the bridge referred to was nearly opposite The Old Leather Bottle, and that the "Deritend Brook" was one which ran nearly parallel with Digbeth, across Rea Street, and into the river Rea near the present stone bridge. The extract is remarkable, not only as an example of the loss of a stream and the removal of a bridge, where accidents frequently occurred, but as indicating the locality of the warehouse of Messrs Humphreys—one of whom lived at the house at Spark Brook, nearly opposite The Angel Inn, when it was attacked in the Riots of 1791.

"On Thursday night last (1789), Mr. Wright, patten-maker, of Digbeth, in this town, attempting to cross the small bridge, over Deritend Brook, opposite Messrs. Humphrey's warehouse, unfortunately fell into the brook; and though the water was but low, yet as he was aged and infirm, and no assistance being nigh, he was incapable of getting out, and was found dead in the mud the next morning. As several persons have fallen over this bridge in the night, we hope some kind of railing will be immediately erected on its sides, or other means adopted, to prevent similar accidents."

The next extract, twenty years later, shows a much more pleasant locality than our present associations lead us to expect. Whatever the "beautiful waterfall" may have been, the "large reservoir" was evidently the Deritend Pool, now completely covered with a net-work of new streets.

"Eligible Tavern AND Pubic Gardens, CALLED Spring Gardens.—To be disposed of by private Treaty, by Mr. Terry, the Good-will and Establishment of this Eligible Concern, carried on with success near 20 years, Situate on the South-East Borders of the town of Birmingham, fronting the beautiful Waterfall on the River Rea, commanding very cheerful and picturesque Views over a large Reservoir and its adjacent fertile Meadows. The Gardens are now in a high state of perfection, lined with Plane sad Lyme Trees, and a beautiful variety of Shrubs, and adorned by several emblematical Figures in Statuary; the Walks well gravelled, and the whole surrounded by various painted Alcoves, Arbours, Reduits a Boire, to accommodate at least One Thousand Persons. The Out-homes ore numerous and excellently arranged, and the Premises throughout are in complete Order and Repair.

"ASSINDER'S TRIPE HOUSE, DIGBETH, AND PART OF OLD HOUSE, BULL STREET."

The subjects of the next Illustration require a few introductory remarks. The former is another fine example of the old houses of Birmingham—ones adorning this old part of the town, but long ago replaced by modern "fronts." This house, like the Old Crown, has happily fallen into the hands of a proprietor who takes a pride in it, and will allow no pulling down, during his own life at least. A large number of deeds concerning this house are in the hands of Mr. Mercer, its owner, but they are not known to contain any important facts. The singular small "part of a house in Bull Street" was one of the most remarkable pieces of building in Bull Street, and was pulled down in December, 1865. It was probably built on an appropriated piece of land—the ancient "eavesdropping," or space between two houses; but in the absence of any definite information, this sketch of what only one in a hundred ever noticed—although it has only just been removed—must be left to tell its own tale as a unique piece of street architecture.

THE GOLDEN LION, DERITEND - c1830

TRIPE HOUSE, DIGBETH & HOUSE IN BULL ST. - c1830

"THE HOLLOWAY HEAD TAVERN AND TEA GARDENS"—

Taking the buildings roughly in the order of their date rather than their locality or associations—is a curious example of an old Birmingham road-side inn, like the Prince Rupert's Head Quarters at Camp Hill. The conical building at the back represents the long-familiar but deserted windmill, so long the evening resort of all classes of "old Brums," but subsequently converted into a sort of Observatory, and now dilapidated, deserted, and despised. The view from the top of this windmill (rarely ascended now) was once very charming, and is even now very interesting; but the glory of the gardens has departed, and the once pleasant suburb "near Birmingham" (as the old advertisements say) has become commonplace and condemned. What the neighbourhood was in 1780, and much later, the following advertisement will show

*"Situated near Bath Row, fronting the lower road leading from Birmingham to the Five Ways. *In a most agreeable situation: the Gardens (the soil whereof is in the highest condition) are planted with espalier and other good Fruit Trees, very famous Gooseberry Trees and Strawberry Beds; also 6 large Asparagus Beds, which yield very plentiful Crops. There is a Back-Way to the Premises from Suffolk-street, a pleasant Walk through the Fields in the Spring and Summer Seasons."*

DOG & DUCK TAVERN, HOLLOWAY HEAD - c1830

"THE OLD SHIP INN, CAMP HILL,"

Marks one of the historic sites of Birmingham, and has been described by the present proprietor, Mr. Turner, in a recent pamphlet, with commendable zeal. Whether "Prince Rupert's Head Quarters" or not, the house is a very old one, and was probably a road side inn in the 1500's. At the end of the 1700's it was known as The Anchor, and Mr. Turner (who is very familiar with "old Birmingham") has collected some curious details of the house he inhabits, in his little book on its history and age.

The original half-timbered farm building, with stables, barn and dairy was a stop for coaches and wagons on the route to Birmingham. The "Bord" - the parish pound, that used to hold stray animals until they were claimed by their owners, was situated alongside the building.

The "Anchor" was into its 70s when Civil War broke out in England and in 1643 the building was, according to the heading over the front entrance, used as Prince Rupert's headquarters in April of that year, whilst he burned many of the buildings of Birmingham during the "Battle of Birmingham", fought on Easter Monday, 3rd of April 1643. The "Anchor" was reputed to be a favourite resort of the Eighteenth Century English Labouring-Class Poet, John Freeth and his friends in the late 1700s, they become known as the 12 Apostles.

"THE PRISON"

(Or the Dungeon) in Peck Lane, was in one of those streets which the New Street Railway Station swept away. The front faced Peck Lane, which entered New Street west of King Edward's School, through the ground now the open space between the School and the Exchange. The street on the left was Pinfold Street, leading into Navigation Street; and the site of the Gaol—the materials of which were sold 28th November, 1806, for £250—was very near the site where the Madras School subsequently stood. The prison-like look of the place made it famous in local memory, and it has been immortalized in a sarcastic triplet referring to one of the latest wakes and "bull-baitings," when the authorities of the day—

"They spoiled the wake,
And stole the stake,
And took the bull to the Dungeon."

"THE POST OFFICE, NEW STREET,"

Represents the building which, for some years, served this growing town as the place for the arrival and departure of the mails. The building was between Temple Street and Bennett's Hill, or, rather, the road which was subsequently formed under that name, and the mail coaches started from the yard behind. A building was afterwards used at the west corner of Bennett's Hill and New Street, and the following extracts will show how postal communications were accomplished in our grandfathers' young days

"Post Office, Birmingham, 4th July, 1787.—The Public are hereby informed that on and after Monday next, the 9th instant, the London Mail Coach will be dispatched from hence at Three o'clock to the Afternoon. All Letters put into this Office before Two will experience that Day's Conveyance—Francis Freeling, Samuel Woodcock, Christopher Sanderland."

"A further extension of Mr. Palmer's Post Plan having taken place between Birmingham and Bristol, the Public are hereby informed, that on and after Friday next, the 6th instant, they will have a daily Communication with all those places the Letters for which have heretofore been sent 3 times a week only by the West Post. The Coach will arrive here every Morning at Nine o'Clock, and its departure from hence will be at Five o'Clock in the Evening.— Francis Freeling, Samuel Woodcock, Christopher Sanderland."

"The Birmingham and Bristol Mail Coach sets off from the Castle Inn, Birmingham, and the Rommer Tavern, Bristol, and stops at the Cross, Bromsgrove, the Star and Garter, Worcester, the Hop Pole, Tewkesbury, the Swan, Gloucester, and the Crown, Newport."

ST. PHILIP'S CHURCH

Forms so prominent an object in this plate illustrating the post office, that it will afford an opportunity of introducing some extracts which give a very graphic picture of the condition of central Birmingham during the last ten years of the last century. The rural attractions, the low rental, the amusements, and the perils of the time require no further reference to be fully understood

"Rus in Urbe (1798)—To be Let, and may be entered upon immediately, Bennett's Hill House and Premises, fronting Newhall Street, to Birmingham, an eligible and commanding Situation; the house consists of 3 Parlors on the Ground Floor, with a suitable number of Bed Rooms, capital Cellaring, Laundry, etc., together with a Coach-house, Stabling for 5 Horses, Granary, Saddle-houses, etc., etc., an extensive Garden and Walks, and any quantity of land not exceeding 4 Acres, which surrounds the same, and may be had therewith, or otherwise, at the Option of the Tenant. The above Premises may be had for any Term of Years, not exceeding twenty."

"To be Sold, and entered upon at lady Day next, a large Messuage or Dwelling House, situated in Temple Street, Birmingham, in the Possession of Mr. Charles Magenis, containing twelve Yards in the Front, four Rooms on a Floor, sashed and fronted both to the Street and Garden, good Cellaring and Vaults, Brewhouse and Stable, with an entire Garden, walled, and the Walls covered with Fruit Trees, the Garden 12 yards, wide, and 50 yards, long from the Front of the House, and extending 22 yards wide for 26 yards further, together with a pleasant Terrace-Walk, and Summer Houses with Sash'd Windows and Sash'd Door adjoining to the open Fields, and commanding a Prospect of four Miles distance, and all necessary Conveniences. Likewise another House in the same Street, in the Tenure of Mr. George Orton, with large Shops, Gardens and Summer House, pleasantly situated, commanding a good Prospect, and set at nine Pounds and ten Shillings per annum.

THE PRISON - 1802

THE POST OFFICE, NEW STREET - c1820

ST PHILIP'S CHURCH

"Birmingham, 24 April, 1780.—There will be a Ball by the Young Ladies and Gentlemen under the Care and Tuition of Mr. Mackorkell, in the Hotel Assembly-Room, on Wednesday, the 17th of May, consisting of the ordinary Minuet; between which will be occasionally introduced Minuet de la Cour, which will end in a lively Dance, called la Gigue Vivant, Minuet Dauphin, which will also end with la Gigue Lasserlane; the Louvre, Rigadoon, Allemand, Cotillions, and a variety of other genteel Dances; and a Ballet Dance. The Scholar's Performance will finish with a Country Dance after which will be a Dance for the Ladies and Gentlemen. The Ball will be opened at 5 o'Clock at Night. Tickets, at 3s. 6d. each, may be had of the Printers, and of Mr. Mackorkell, at Mr. Farror's, in the Bull Ring. He begs to subjoin his most sincere thanks to his Friends in general, for the genteel Encouragement he has already met with, and assures them it shall be his principal Object to pay the greatest Attention to the Behavior and Improvement of his Pupils."

"Between eight and nine o'clock on Friday night (December, 1792), as a Lady of this town, with her footman and a lantern before her, was passing along St. Philip's Church Yard, she was attacked, with horrid imprecations, in the walk from the Blue School to the Rev. Mr. Madan's, by two men, who ran violently against her, and tore her clothes; and but for the spirit of her footman, she would inevitably have been the victim of their villainous designs."

Work on the building of St Philips Church commenced in 1709 and it was one of the first new parish churches to be built after the Reformation. Its architect was Thomas Archer. William Westley who created the first plan of Birmingham, surveyed in 1731, is also credited for laying wooden floors and erecting the gallery during its completion in 1715, the year it was consecrated. The tower remained uncompleted until 1725 due to a lack of funding.

It's All Gone

A reflection on the sketches of Birmingham from Volume One
Poem by Ian Henery

The half-timbered houses in Deritend,
Their pretty suburbs were to me like friends:
Ornaments and honours of this great town,
The gabled property called The Old Crown.
The Golden Lion has gone and pretty streets,
In Deritend, where we used to meet.
Where are the famous buildings of old time?
Where have they gone and what was their crime?
I can't find Birmingham.

What has happened to the little Spark Brook?
I have searched for it but its not in books.
A tributary of the River Rea,
How can a stream just vanish - disappear?
Completely covered up and lined with trees,
A site of warehouses, Messrs Humphreys.
The Deritend Brook has also vanished,
In the way of progress, so was banished.
I can't find Birmingham.

Digbeth's Tripe House, another departure,
An example of street architecture.
Also gone, the Holloway Head tavern
Called The Dog & Duck, a drinking cavern.
It used to be a famous roadside inn,
Always had a warm welcome within
And at the back, a deserted windmill,
Views over fertile fields and watermills.
I can't find Birmingham.

It's all gone, dilapidated and despised,
Beauty has been stolen, replaced with lies.
Views from the windmill's top were full of charms,
Promises whispered in my sweetheart's arms.
The poetry of that place departed,
Leaving me bereft and broken hearted.
Once pleasant suburbs are now commonplace,
Condemned, deserted and sadly defaced.
I can't find Birmingham.

Near Bath Row, the route leading to Five Ways,
There were planted gardens where we once played:
Gooseberry bushes and strawberry beds,
We stopped awhile and rested weary heads.
Six large asparagus beds and fruit trees,
Confetti for us, honey for the bees.
Pleasant walks in spring and summer seasons,
Together, we did not need a reason.
I can't find Birmingham.

Suffolk Street offered views of rural life;
Low rents when you said you would be my wife.
Good soil in the meadows, plentiful crops;
They have all been covered up with new shops.
On each building are signs of trades displayed,
Manufacturing bolts, bricks, nails and spades.
Our Garden was replaced by higher rents,
The Paradise gone, other amusements.
I can't find Birmingham.

The old Ship Inn was a historic site
At Camp Hill, where Prince Rupert spent the night.
The Royal Navy's flag was flown above,
A roadside inn that we all came to love,
A place to eat and our spirits to heal;
But pulled down by town developer's zeal:
Demolished, our tavern, our lovely place
And it's all gone, removed without a trace.
I can't find Birmingham.

Gone the old prison that stood in Peck Lane,
No tears were shed, no souvenirs remain.
It was pulled down for the New Street Railway,
Dismantled by progress and swept away.
Famous in local memory, no more
Consigned to history, the rule of law.
Birmingham's prison, our lock-up, our gaol,
Criminals in handcuffs seen through the rails.
I can't find Birmingham.

New Street's Post Office can cover the land,
Growing sacks of mail delivered by hand.
Our mail coaches now unite the nation,
Letters a daily communication.
Out of London, the mail men set their course
For a warm coach house and stable for horse,
A welcome retreat from the dusty road
When carrying the post, a precious load.
I can't find Birmingham.

Where is Pinfold Street? It was "The City",
The landmark was a shared identity.
A narrow old lane, the leases expired,
Pulled like rotten teeth, no longer desired.
Absent in New Street are the whip makers,
Garden at the front, next door to bakers:
All pulled out, an increase in land value,
Filled with shops, no time for a pretty view.
I can't find Birmingham.

Dale End, The Old Engine was also doomed:
A new railway bridge meant it was entombed
By progress - with no time for the flowers
And friendship spent in once convivial hours?
All the places we once shared together,
Our Birmingham, no matter the weather.
They have all gone, retired from their labours,
These lovely buildings lost to their neighbours.
I can't find Birmingham.

Smallbrook Street was the route to Edgbaston,
Through meadows it stretched to the horizon;
This fine abode of aristocracy,
Birmingham now a meritocracy.
Gentle Worcester Street, once called Swan Alley,
Where we caroused and performed our ballet,
Flattened, like the levelling of Hurst Hill,
Renamed Hurst Street and our reservoir filled.
I can't find Birmingham.

Birmingham's High Street and Court of Requests,
Changed by bankers with money to invest.
The fine metal work with vertical spouts,
Were all sold off to a banker with gout.
The Court of Requests is now empty, disused,
A handsome Queen Anne building that's abused;
For this, if you want to know who to thank
Let me whisper - Attwood's & Spooner's Bank.
I can't find Birmingham.

All buildings have a soul, they have a heart,
A fact forgotten when they're torn apart;
Pulled out like teeth, prised open like a shell,
The sylvan paradise we knew so well.
Birmingham is my home, it's in my blood,
I have been away and it's changed for good
And for the better? You must all now decide:
Our Birmingham, our town, our civic pride.

"PINFOLD STREET"

Represents that narrow old lane formerly known as "THE CITY," the upper part of the plate representing the houses pretty much as they stand now—but threatened with removal before long, as the leases expire, and new and

more commanding buildings occupy the site. The lower drawing represents that part of the street destroyed by the railway alterations, and nearly coincident with the present line of Queen Street, or Great Queen Street, as it was generally called, till the memory of the original and demolished Queen Street was finally lost.

"THE WHIP MANUFACTORY, NEW STREET,"

Shows an old familiar block of building pulled down last year (1865), and showing very remarkably the increased value of land. When originally built the premises stood back from the street and, like many others of the houses in New Street, had a garden before them. In due time, however, the front space was utilised by shops, while the old portions behind were used as warehouses and workshops for one of the great old Birmingham trades.

"THE HOUSES AT THE BOTTOM OF PINFOLD STREET"

This sketch shows the buildings at the left hand corner of the upper plate of Pinfold Street (page 32) on a large scale, as well as the ascent towards Christ Church Schools and Ann Street. The left of the picture shows a part of Navigation Street, destroyed by the Stour Valley crossing, and the present railway bridge.

"DALE END, CORNER OF MOOR STREET,"

Will be readily recognised as still existing, but also doomed. The Dale End frontages rather different now from its appearance when this sketcb was made —a wooden frame-work having been erected some years ago, partly hiding the dormer-window in the roof.

CHRIST CHURCH

"THE OLD ENGINE, DALE END,"

Represents an old inn, still remarkable for 'the "engine" under one of the dormer-windows, from which the name is derived. The "old engine" has long rested from its labors, but thirty years ago it was occasionally worked by a smoke-jack in the adjoining chimney, and formed a very attractive and remarkable inn sign. Not far from here, as late as 1792, there was a "Pound," where not only stray cattle, but goods were taken, as there is a record of "A Cask" in the Pound.

"WORCESTER STREET, CORNER OF EDGBASTON STREET,"

Will be easily recognised, although the building of forty years ago has been replaced by a cheap and, evidently, "short-lease" structure. The portion of the house on the right is one of those comfortable old homes which were once the abodes of our aristocracy, when Smallbrook Street was the road "leading from Birmingham to Edgbaston," and when Holloway Head was not filled up, which operation was accomplished in 1792. The higher end of Worcester Street—then known as Swan Alley—was crossed by an archway, and a similar arch or gate existed in Smallbrook Street, near Hurst Street, which latter seems to have taken its name from "Hurst Hill," although no trace of the "Hill" remains.

"DUDLEY STREET,"

Another of the doomed streets shortly to be sacrificed to town improvements— will be easily recognised by every reader of these lines, and need not be further described, as no historic associations are connected with it, except that, as late as 1793, a resident of the adjoining "Hinklys" advertised his school as being in a pleasant locality and affording a good education to the boys of seventy years ago.

WHIP MANUFACTORY, NEW ST. - c1830

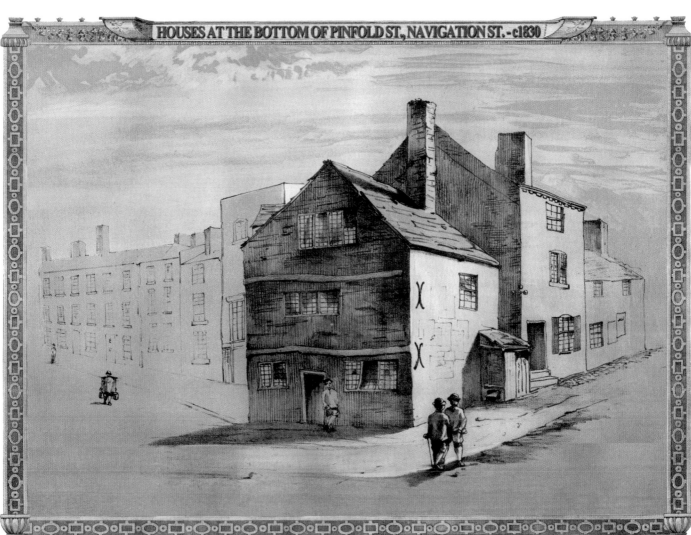

HOUSES AT THE BOTTOM OF PINFOLD ST, NAVIGATION ST. - c1830

DALE END, CORNER OF MOOR ST. - c1830

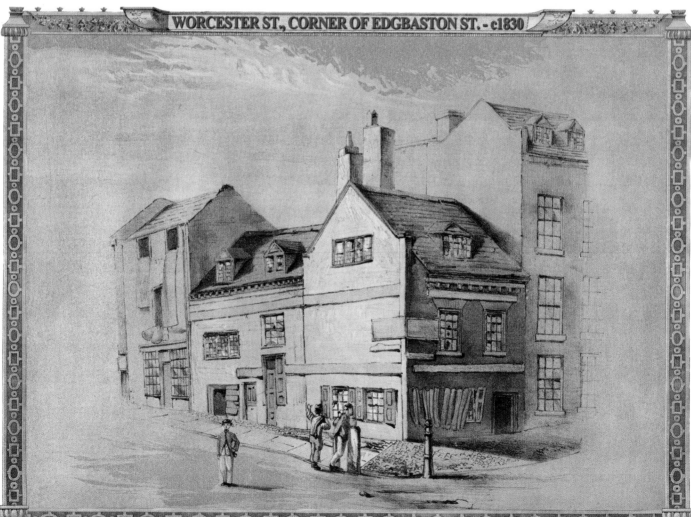

WORCESTER ST., CORNER OF EDGBASTON ST. - c1830

THE OLD ENGINE, DALE END – C1830

DUDLEY STR

"BULL STREET, CORNER OF CROOKED LANE,"

Represents another of those old shops of Birmingham soon to be replaced by the loftier and more imposing edifices of modern days. The building left of the Crooked Lane occupies the site of a rather famous place—an old house which stood back from the street, and was in late years fronted by a liquor shop, and held for many years by J. P. LUCAS, a droll and dry old auctioneer, whose ready wit and frequent sarcasm were often displayed while selling "everybody's rubbish," which, he said, was the business of his life.

"HIGH STREET AND COURT OF REQUESTS"

Show some street architecture still outstanding as it has done for nearly two hundred years. The vertical spouts are especially remarkable as fine examples of the metal work of the year marked upon them, 1687. The Court of Requests, now long disused for the recovery of small debts, is a handsome building of Queen Anne's days, and has gained more than a merely local fame from William Hutton's most curious and amusing work detailing his experience as a Commissioner of that Court. The shrewd common sense, the impartial decisions, and the dry humour displayed in his record of the "Cases" he decided, are very amusing and very instructive too. The worthy old Historian declares that when his house in High Street (nearly opposite the end of New Street, on the site now marked as "Hutton's Place") was attacked in the Riots of 1791, the mob was urged on by those against whom be had decided as a Commissioner of the neighbouring Court.

"NEW STREET AND CORNER OF WORCESTER STREET,"

Where the gateway, already mentioned, spanned the latter street, is a memorial of a lofty house recently removed to "round the corner" and improve the approaches and facilitate the increasing traffic of the busiest part of Birmingham. This important "improvement" is a remarkable example of the increased value of land in Birmingham—the cost of the improvement, including the land and compensations, having been £14,246, or nearly £60 a yard, and the remaining land having been sold for £18,360, or *£30* per yard.

"ATTWOOD AND SPOONER'S BANK"

Is a sketch of the present building, made before the disastrous failure had associated such unpleasant recollections with the two well-known names.

In concluding this brief Introduction to these pictorial records of The Buildings of Birmingham Past and Present, the writer may be allowed to add that the subject is far from exhausted, and that much very interesting matter might have been added to these brief notes if the nature of the work had allowed a full description of the old buildings of the town. The history of public buildings is pretty easily obtained; but places like those delineated in this work are in so many hands and their history is often so obscure that it is hopeless to attempt a complete, exhaustive account. Any details which can still be given relating to these or any other old buildings in our town, will be very thankfully received by the publisher of this work, which will probably be followed by the publication of other sketches illustrating the history of the streets and buildings of our good old town.

Samuel Timmins, Birmingham, January 1866.

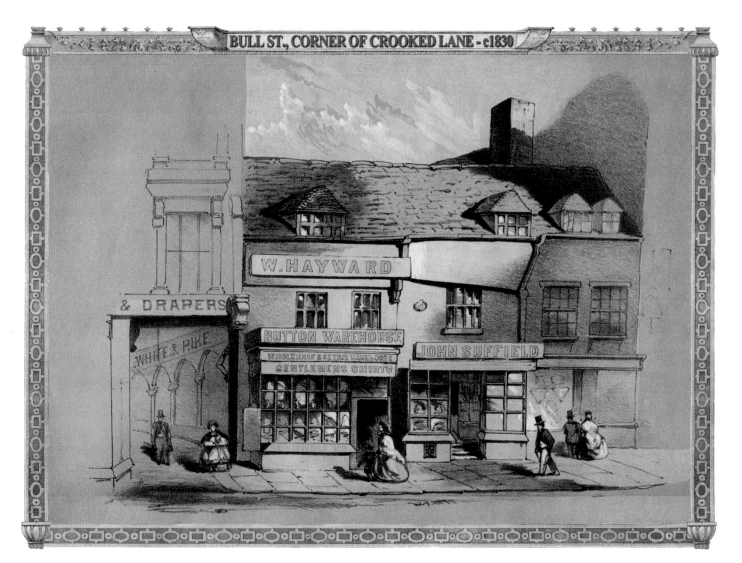

BULL ST., CORNER OF CROOKED LANE - c1830

& DRAPERS

WHITE & PIKE

W. HAYWARD

BUTTON WAREHOUSE

WHOLESALE & RETAIL WAREHOUSE

GENTLEMENS SHIRTS

JOHN SUFFIELD

HIGH ST. & COURT OF REQUESTS - c1830

THE GREAT AMERICAN
CRINOLINE
AND STAY FACTORY

32

OAKLEY & BENNETT

LATE

WALKER & STAINES

31

30

PALE ALE
& STOUT

HENRY SPENCER.

DEALERS IN TEA.

30½
REDFERN

I & F. LLOYD & Co

HORTON   29   HORTON

HORTON

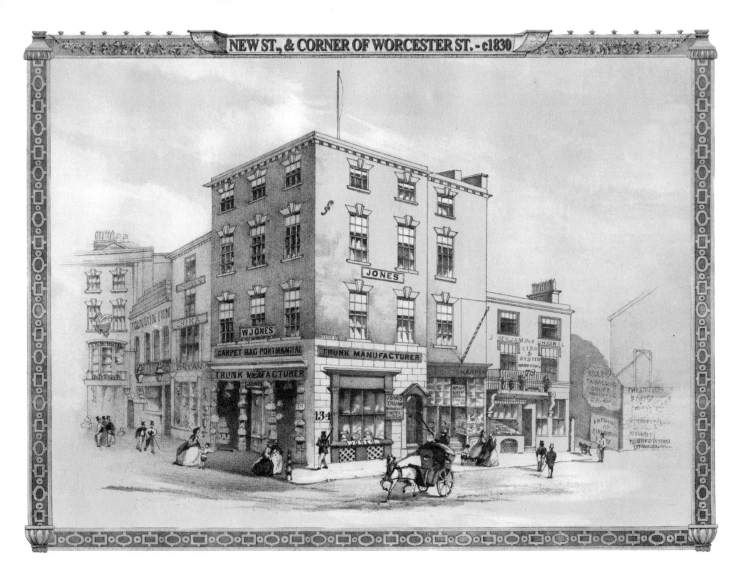

NEW ST., & CORNER OF WORCESTER ST. - c1830

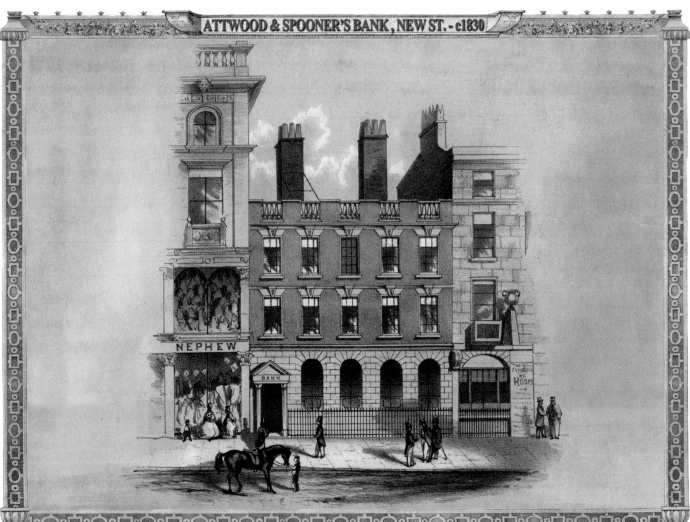

ATTWOOD & SPOONER'S BANK, NEW ST. - c1830

MANUFACTURING TRADE PLATES

Samuel Timmins 'The Birmingham and Midland Hardware district' (1866) contains the most detailed description of the trades in operation in the town during this period. Willey's 'History and Guide to Birmingham' (1868) states the following:

"The manufactures of Birmingham are almost infinite in their variety. Almost all articles of utility or ornament are manufactured in the town. From a pin to a steam engine, from pens to swords and guns, from "cheap and nasty" wares sold at country fairs by "cheap Johns" to the exquisitely beautiful and elaborate gold and silver services which adorn mansions of the rich … all things are made in this hive of industry, and give employment to its thousands of men, women, and children".

The Copper Engravings of a Lost World
(Manufacturing Trade Plates)
(Sonnet) by Ian Henery

Birmingham's manufacturing trade plates
Are a glimpse of adverts from yesteryear:
Ostrich plumes, foreign wines and Dudley beer;
Shoe scrapers, vases, ink stands and fire grates,
Hurdles or plain and ornamental gates.
Leather goods for the Royal Family,
Teas from the East India Company,
Goods we still buy and some now out of date.

These engravings are a lost catalogue
Of fashion in the Victorian Age;
They speak out to us from history's page,
Of tea and coffee dealers and brass cogs;
Boots, shoes, saddles, andirons and firedogs.
Look at the pictures -New Street without cars!
Carriages and taverns instead of bars,
A lost and naïve world by travelogue.

KENDALL & SON,
AT THE
CIVET CAT, №447, WEST STRAND,
LONDON.

PERFUMERS, CABINET CASE MAKERS,
and Importers of Foreign Fancy Merchandise &c.&c.
TO THE ROYAL FAMILY.

BRANCHES.	WHOLESALE WAREHOUSES.
№17, New Street, Birmingham.	№1, Adelaide St. Charing Cross, London.
№18, Foregate Street, Worcester.	№49, Lombard Street, Birmingham.
№35, Market Street, Manchester.	AGENTS.
№61, Lord Street, Liverpool.	Thos Spring & Company, Exeter.
№63, Wine Street, Bristol &c.&c.	B.S. Wilks & Company, Dublin.

Published by Radclyffes & Co. for their History of Birmingham & its Vicinity.

MARTINEAU & SMITH,

PATENTEES OF THE CORK BARREL COCK.

BRASS COCK FOUNDERS AND GENERAL FACTORS, 65 HILL STREET, BIRMINGHAM.

T. Radclyffe, Sc.

Published by Radclyffes & Co. for their History of Birmingham & its Vicinity.

I. R. ANDREWS,
TEA & COFFEE DEALER,
Nº 14, HIGH STREET, BIRMINGHAM.

The Teas sold at this Establishment are bought by a Broker, at the East India Company's Sales, and are sold out to the Public, at the same prices, & profits, as are usually charged to the Trade, by the London Wholesale dealers. BEING A SAVING OF NEARLY TEN PER CENT TO THE CONSUMER.

Published by Radclyffes & Cº for their History of Birmingham & its Vicinity   T.Radclyffe Sc.

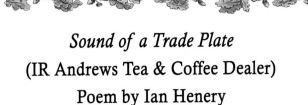

Sound of a Trade Plate
(IR Andrews Tea & Coffee Dealer)
Poem by Ian Henery

"A saving of nearly 10% to the consumer!"
The engraving proudly exclaims,
Teas being bought by a broker
In the East India Company.
It is sold to the public -
There then follows a confusing spiel
About London wholesalers,
Profits and prices
But all I can see
Are vast, sweeping skies
Above Birmingham:
No

*   telegraph poles*
*   blocks of flats*
*   or motorway bridges.*
*   No Rotunda,*
*   No Mailbox*
*   (was life worth living?)*
*   or mobile phone masts.*

I listen for the sound
The trade plates makes in my soul:
I hear excited children,
Ladies haggling for bargains
In the High Street's market
And human laughter
Without the ever-pounding roar
Of cars rushing headlong on motorways
And motorbikes revving in anticipation.
I hear the scream of aeroplanes
Rushing to somewhere else
*   somewhere preferable*
*   somewhere more interesting*
*   somewhere that is nowhere,*
*   An escape from now*
*   And loneliness,*
*   this reality of*
*   being*
*   Here.*

Is anywhere better than here,
This precious moment in time?
I close my eyes and listen:
Birmingham without deafening traffic,
Where people can experience reality
And actually listen to themselves
Without stimuli bombardment.
I hear a man with a placard and bowler hat
Inviting ladies to the tea and coffee dealer,
A cup of magic on the High Street
In Victorian Birmingham.

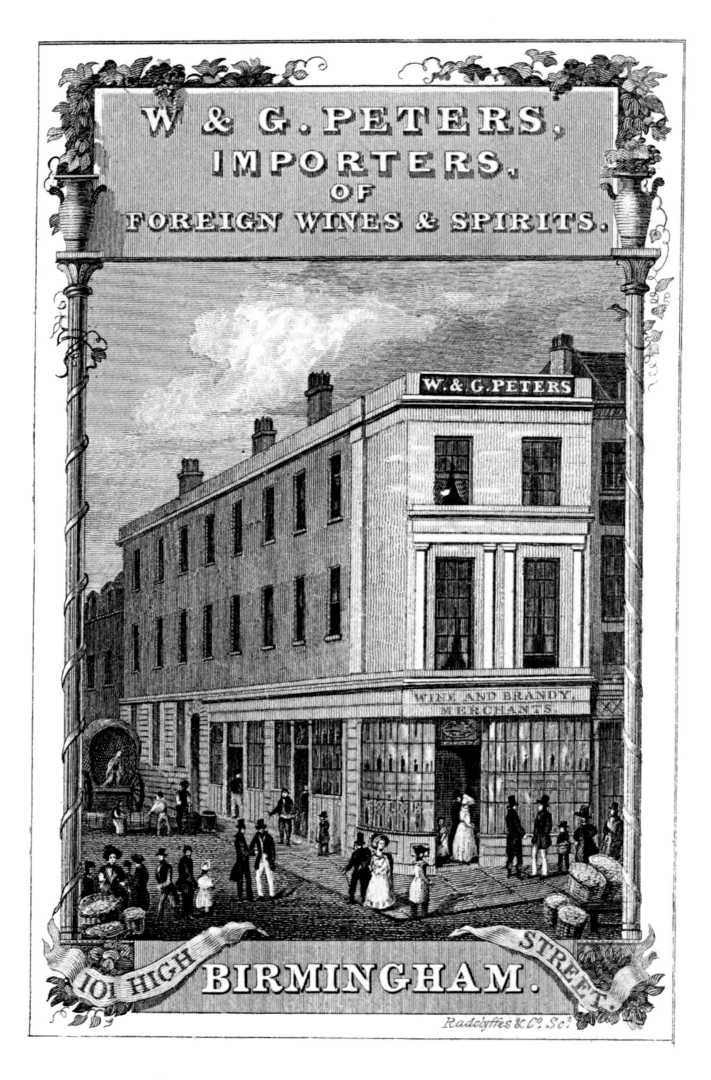

W & G. PETERS,
IMPORTERS,
OF
FOREIGN WINES & SPIRITS.

W. & G. PETERS

WINE AND BRANDY
MERCHANTS

101 HIGH STREET
BIRMINGHAM.

Radclyffes & Co. Sc.

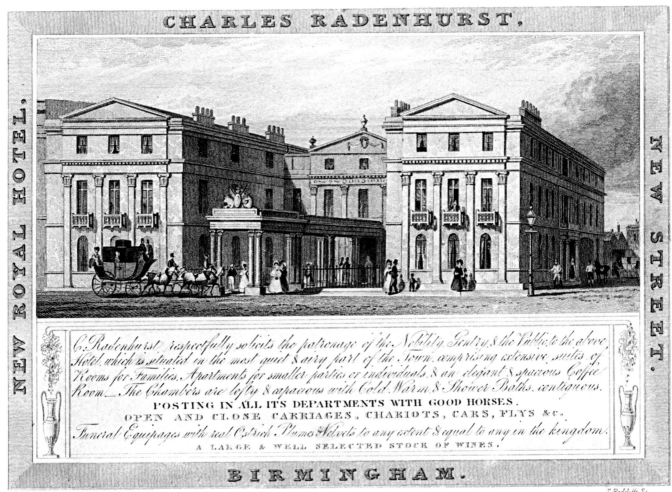

The New Royal Hotel
Poem by Ian Henery

Come to Birmingham's New Royal hotel
In New Street, a quiet part of town;
Patronage sought from persons of renown,
Comprising extensive airy suites in pastel
Refined decor, each room with an inkwell,
Lofty chambers every one perfumed.
We have shower baths and the Coffee Room,
We provide luxury and in that we excel

The New Royal Hotel, its elegance
With its banqueting suite in which to dine,
A large and selected stock of wine,
Trademark of the Hotel is excellence.
We provide for patrons of importance
And stable good horses for carriages:
Host funerals and happy marriages,
All covered whatever the preferences.

49

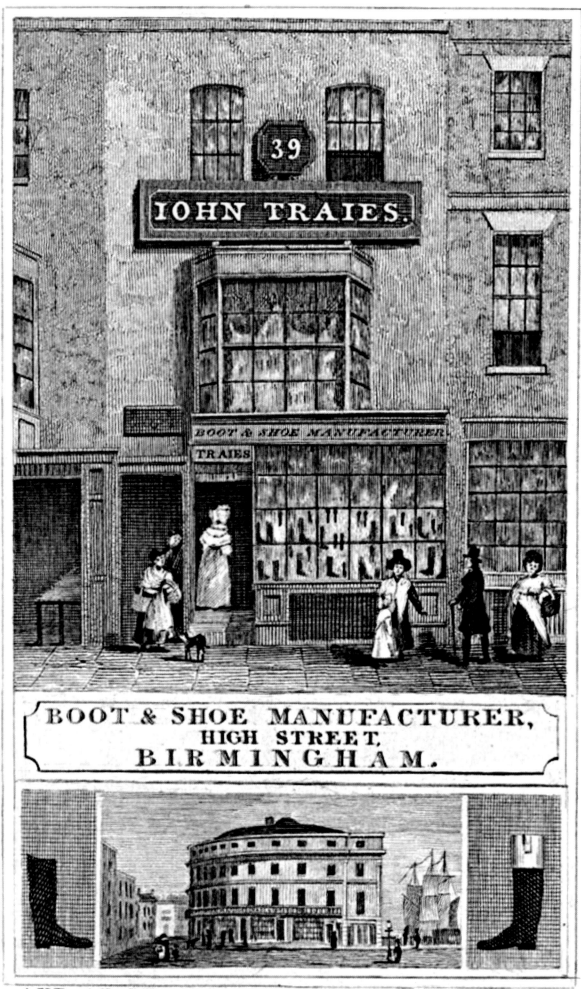

39

IOHN TRAIES.

BOOT & SHOE MANUFACTURER

TRAIES

BOOT & SHOE MANUFACTURER,
HIGH STREET,
BIRMINGHAM.

AND AT 9 BRIDGE END NEWCASTLE·ON·TYNE.

Radclyffes & Co. Sc.

50

Nº 31.
S. E. CHURCHILL,
OPERATIVE & EXPERIMENTAL CHEMIST,
& Dealer in Cabinet Specimens of Minerals.

Nº 37.
CORNISH'S
CHEAP BOOK ESTABLISHMENT.

Nº 38.
H. JOWETT & Cº
WOOLLEN DRAPERS, TAILORS &c.

Nº 42.
H. JOHNSON,
CHEMIST AND DRUGGIST.

Nº 42.
A. TURNER,
CABINET MAKER AND UPHOLSTERER.

Nº 45 & 46.
J. W. SHOWELL,
PRINTER AND STATIONER.

New Street Birmingham from the West.

Society of Arts.   Theatre. New Royal Hotel.

Nº 52.
PRINTER, LAW STATIONER
JAMES DRAKE,
LAW & GENERAL BOOKSELLER.
AGENT TO THE
Phœnix Fire Office. & to the Society for the Diffusion of useful knowledge.

Nº 70.
MUNDEN & CAMERON,
MUSIC & MUSICAL INSTRUMENT WAREHOUSE,
Adjoining the Society of Arts.

Nº 88.
WILLIAM DANIELL,
LITHOGRAPHER, ENGRAVER & PRINTSELLER,
Opposite the Society of Arts.

Nº 110.
J. P. LUCAS,
AUCTIONEER, APPRAISER & LAND SURVEYOR,
Commissioner for taking Special Bail.

Nº 110.
JAMES SCOTT,
SHARE BROKER AND GENERAL AGENT,
and at Nº 88 Bath Row.

Nº 120.
C. KNIBB,
WOOLLEN DRAPER & CLOTHIER.

Published by Radclyffes & Co. for their History of Birmingham & its Vicinity.   T.Radclyffe sc.

THE DUDLEY BREWERY,

FINE ALE

XXX

T. Radclyffe. Sc.

THOS & JAS UPFILL,

IRON & STEEL WAREHOUSE,
Nº 157, GREAT CHARLES STREET, BIRMINGHAM,
MANUFACTURERS OF

WROUGHT IRON HURDLES, PLAIN & ORNAMENTAL GATES, PILASTERS, PALISADING,
PARK FENCING, TREE GUARDS, STABLE RACKS, MANGERS, GARDEN CHAIRS, WAGGON ARMS,
TIRE, CHAINS & NAILS OF ALL SORTS, CABLE CHAINS, AND IRON WORK IN GENERAL.

T. Radclyffe Sc.

Published by Radclyffes & Co.for their History of Birmingham & its Vicinity.

53

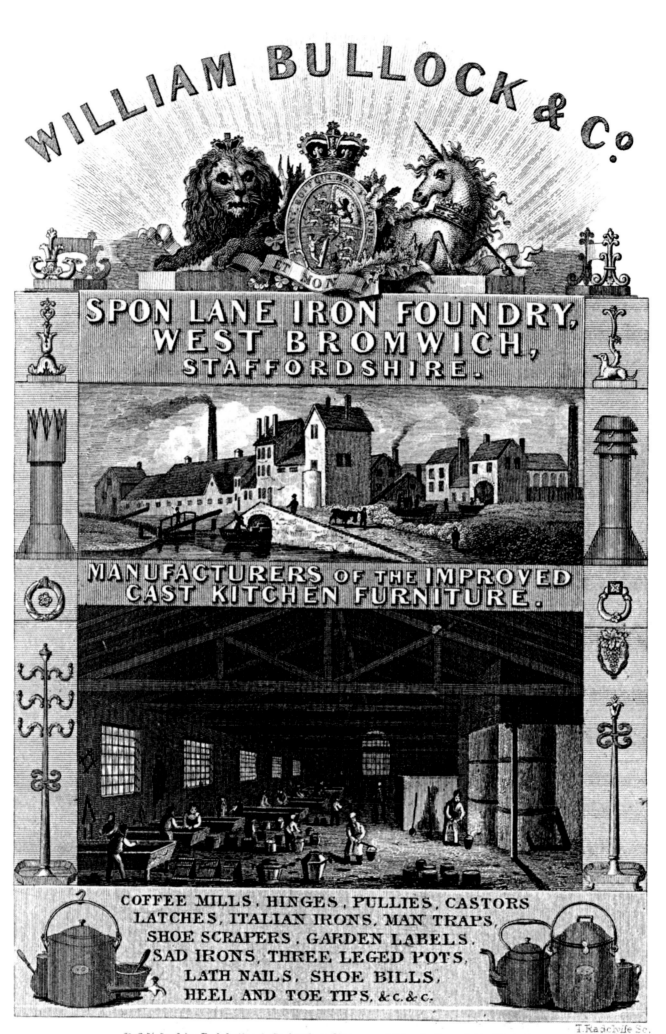

WILLIAM BULLOCK & Co.

SPON LANE IRON FOUNDRY, WEST BROMWICH, STAFFORDSHIRE.

MANUFACTURERS OF THE IMPROVED CAST KITCHEN FURNITURE.

COFFEE MILLS, HINGES, PULLIES, CASTORS
LATCHES, ITALIAN IRONS, MAN TRAPS,
SHOE SCRAPERS, GARDEN LABELS,
SAD IRONS, THREE LEGED POTS,
LATH NAILS, SHOE BILLS,
HEEL AND TOE TIPS, &c.&c.

T. Radclyffe Sc.

Published by Radclyffes & Co. for their History of Birmingham & its Vicinity.

T. RYLAND & SON,
SILVER PLATERS.

40, NEW-HALL STREET,
BIRMINGHAM.

T. Radclyffe Sc.

Published by Radclyffes & Co for their History of Birmingham & its Vicinity.

SIR EDWARD THOMASON,
BIRMINGHAM,
MANUFACTURER OF ARTICLES
IN THE HIGHEST CLASSES OF THE ARTS,
IN GOLD, SILVER, PLATED, OR-MOLU & BRONZE.

T Radclyffe Sc.

Published by Radclyffes & Co. for their History of Birmingham & its Vicinity.

56

JAMES HARRISON,

AUCTIONEER AND SWORN APPRAISER.

COMMERCIAL SALE ROOMS,

NEW STREET, CORNER OF CANNON S.^T

BIRMINGHAM.

SALE ROOM

GENERAL AGENT.

ESTATES SURVEYED AND LEVELS TAKEN.

T. Radclyffe Sc.

Published by Radclyffes and Co. for their History of Birmingham & its Vicinity.

J. DARWEN & SON,
SADDLERS,
HARNESS MAKERS, BRIDLE CUTTERS,
& ARMY ACCOUTREMENT MAKERS,
WHOLESALE & RETAIL;
Nos 7. & 8. EDGBASTON STREET,
BIRMINGHAM.

DIEU ET MON DROIT

HONI SOIT QUI MAL Y PENSE

Thos Radclyffe sc.

Published by Radclyffes & Co for their History of Birmingham & its Vicinity.

58

JOHN BLAKEWAY.

MANUFACTURER OF

LAMPS, CHANDELIERS AND CANDELABRA

BRONZES, INKSTANDS, VASES, &c., &c.

EDGBASTON STREET,

BIRMINGHAM.

Published by Radclyffes & Co. for their History of Birmingham & its Vicinity.

T. Radclyffe sc.

BY SPECIAL APPOINTMENT.

HONI SOIT QUI MALY

DIEU ET MON DROIT

THOMAS ROLLASON,
LATE M. ROLLASON & SON,
MANUFACTURER OF CUT GLASS
TO THE ROYAL FAMILY,
DEALER IN CHINA, EARTHENWARE &c.
STEEL HOUSE LANE,
BIRMINGHAM.

Thos. Radclyffe sc.

Published by Radclyffes & Co. for their History of Birmingham & its Vicinity.

MESSENGER
AND SONS,

MANUFACTURERS
OF
CHANDELIERS,
TRIPODS
AND LAMPS,
OF
EVERY DESCRIPTION
IN BRONZE,
AND OR-MOLU.

BIRMINGHAM
AND
LONDON.

W Green del.   Published by Radclyfes and Co for their History of Birmingham and its Vicinity.   Radclyfe sc.

RADCLYFFES & COMP?

STEEL & COPPER PLATE ENGRAVERS.

GENERAL PRINTERS & STATIONERS.

N°3 PECK LANE
NEW STREET.

BIRMINGHAM.

D.R.Walker. Del.

Radclyffe. Sc.

Published by Radclyffes & Co. for their History of Birmingham & its Vicinity

62

THE MINING & MANUFACTURING DISTRICT

The Mining and Manufacturing District originally engraved by Radclyffe, published in Radclyffe's Birmingham and Its Vicinity as a Manufacturing and Commercial District, 1836, has been re-mastered in full colour for this publication. The full extent of the Coal Basin is distinguished by a continuous purple colour shade, stretching from Stourbridge and Halesowen to north of Cannock. The location of other mineral resources, Lime, Basalt or Rag, as well as Fire Clay is also distinguished with pastel colour. The complex network of canals is by now heavily burdened by the volume of traffic being generated by the burgeoning industry. However, their role in the transportation of resources driving the Industrial Revolution would soon decline rapidly. At the time this map was originally published, railways were already under construction and within the same decade they would be cutting through the Manufacturing Districts linking Birmingham to Liverpool and Manchester, and Birmingham with London.

Heart of the Black Country
Poem by Ian Henery
(i.m. Geoff Stevens)

Does the Black Country's heart beat now?
The winding gears have stopped turning,
No black-faced miners clamber to the surface.
Does the earth spark of industry
Flutter in a dark office drawer?
Does the Black Country's heart beat now?
Has it been trained to come to hand
And sit, songless, like a masked eagle

On a gloved fist of progress
That encircles our towns with dual carriageways
Decorated with meaningless street art?
Does the Black Country's heart beat now,
Stored in a thousand memory banks
Of archived sight and sound?
What pulse from the Black Country's heart
When everything is made in Taiwan?

Where Are the Miners?
(in memory of my Grandpa, George Henery –
coal miner and trade union leader)
Poem by Ian Henery

Where are the miners,
Winding their way back home?
Black-covered faces, calloused hands,
Tunneling deep under the loam,
Digging for coal beneath the land,
Where are the miners?

Where are the miners,
Those legends of Black Country graft?
Wheels of industry keep turning,
Profits must be made down mine shafts
And home fires must be kept burning.
Where are the miners?

Where are the miners?
The world is sterile and clean;
Gone pit ponies and winding gears,
Life`s a bank of computer screens,
Not the chimneys of yesteryear.

Gone are the men black as jet:
They are fossilised like amber,
Embalmed in their tears, blood and sweat,
A legacy few remember.

Forges poured searing streams of gold
Powered by men mining for coal;
Pits of hell, so it could be sold,
Giving their lives in deep, dark holes.

These men ignited foundries,
Casting within our hearts a pride;
Their commitment made industry
But manufacturing has died.
Where are the miners?

Where are the miners?
They have gone - never seen again
But in museums, sight and sound:
Trade union working class men,
Blood on the coal face underground
There are the miners.

Gin Pit

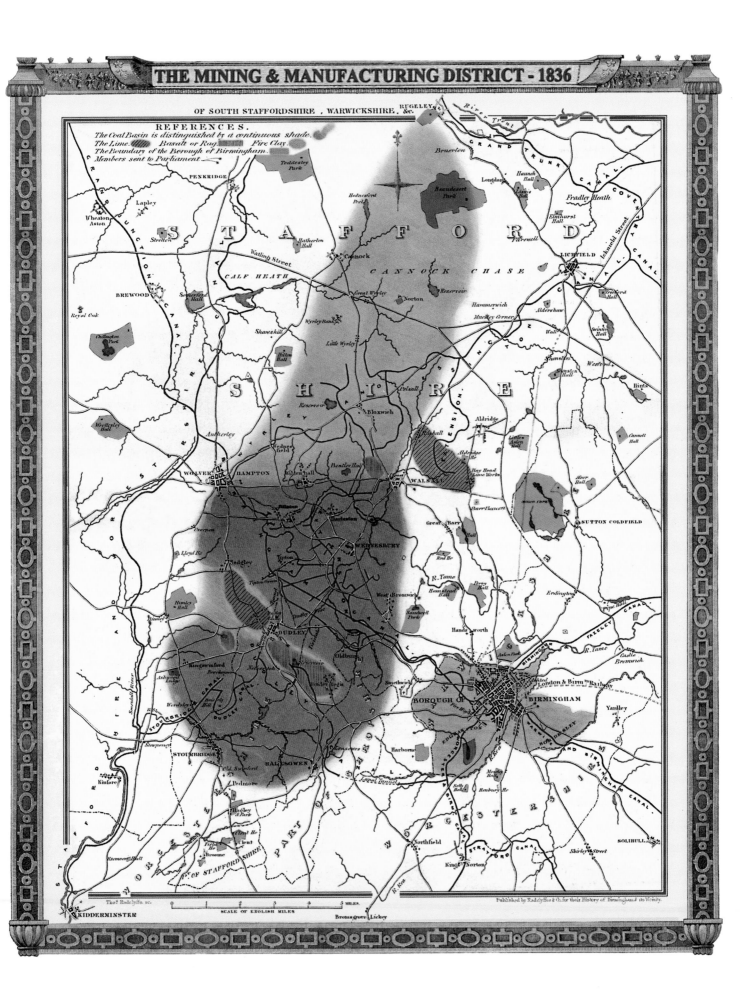

THE MINING & MANUFACTURING DISTRICT - 1836

OF SOUTH STAFFORDSHIRE , WARWICKSHIRE, RUGELEY &c.

REFERENCES.
The Coal Basin is distinguished by a continuous shade.
The Lime.   Basalt or Rag.   Fire Clay.
The Boundary of the Borough of Birmingham.
Members sent to Parliament.

SCALE OF ENGLISH MILES

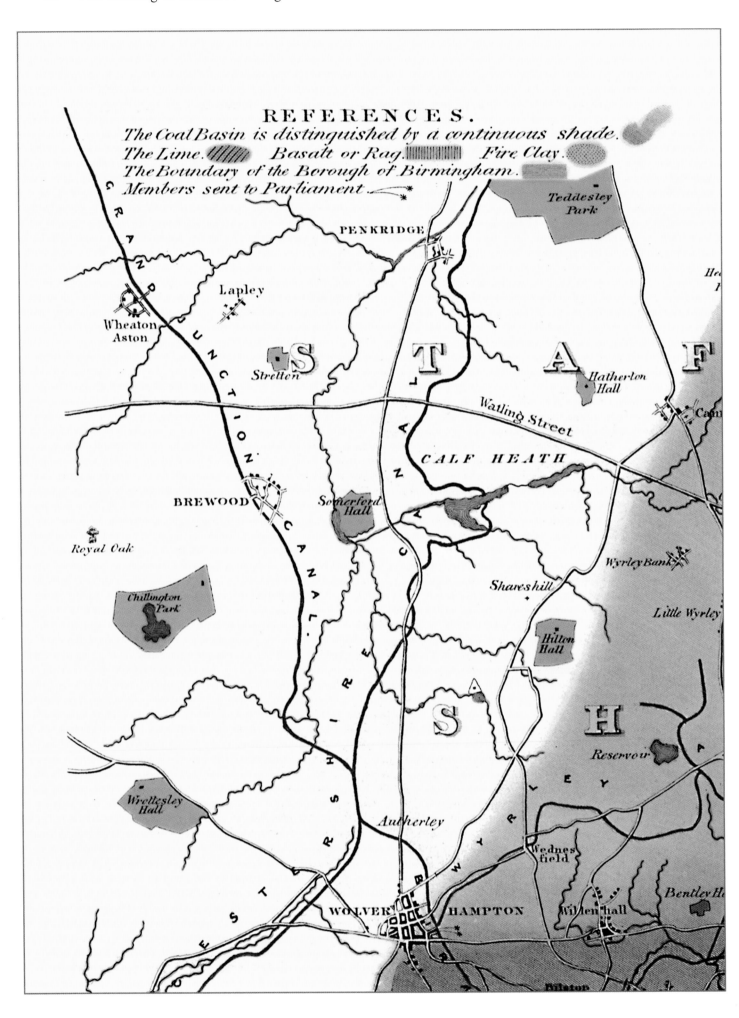

REFERENCES.

The Coal Basin is distinguished by a continuous shade.
The Lime.   Basalt or Rag.   Fire Clay.
The Boundary of the Borough of Birmingham.
Members sent to Parliament.

PENKRIDGE

Teddesley Park

Lapley

Wheaton Aston

Stretton

S   T   A   F

Hatherton Hall

Watling Street

CALF HEATH

BREWOOD

Somerford Hall

Royal Oak

Chillington Park

Shareshill

Wyrley Bank

Little Wyrley

Hilton Hall

S

Reservoir

Wrottesley Hall

Autherley

Wednes-field

WOLVER   HAMPTON   Willenhall   Bentley H

Bilston

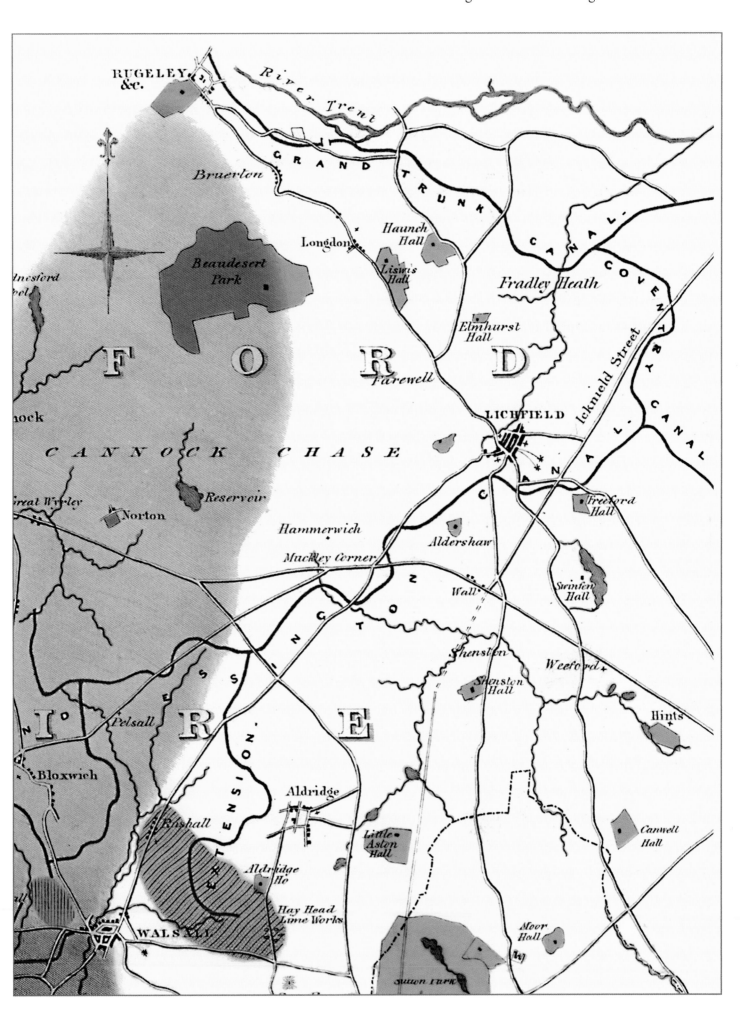

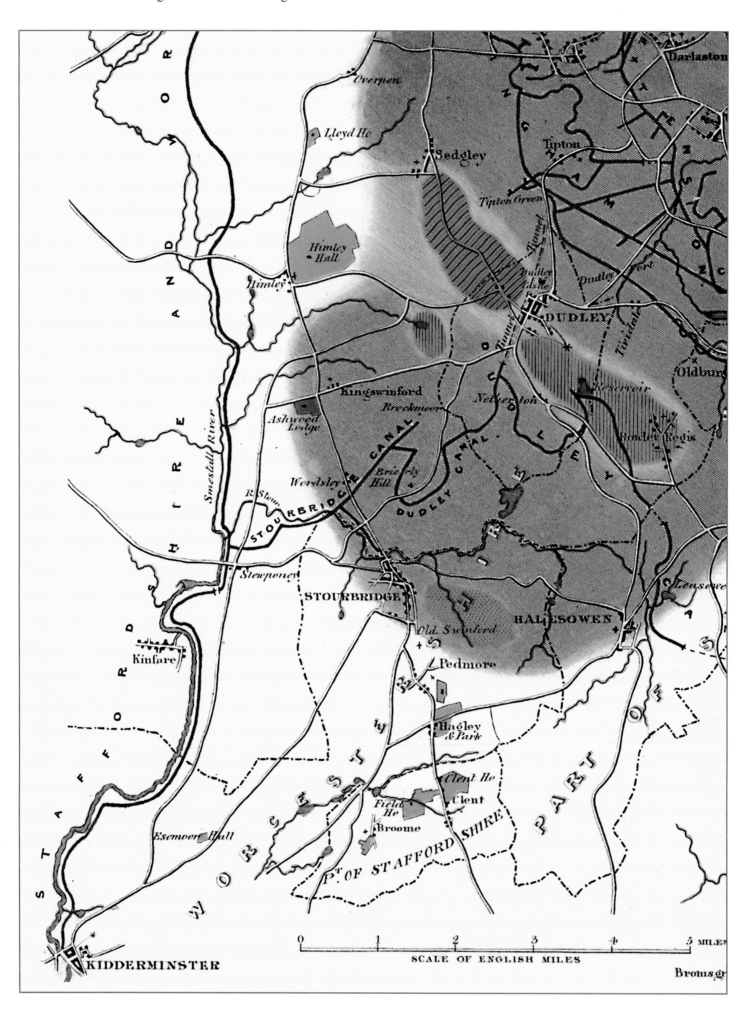

SCALE OF ENGLISH MILES

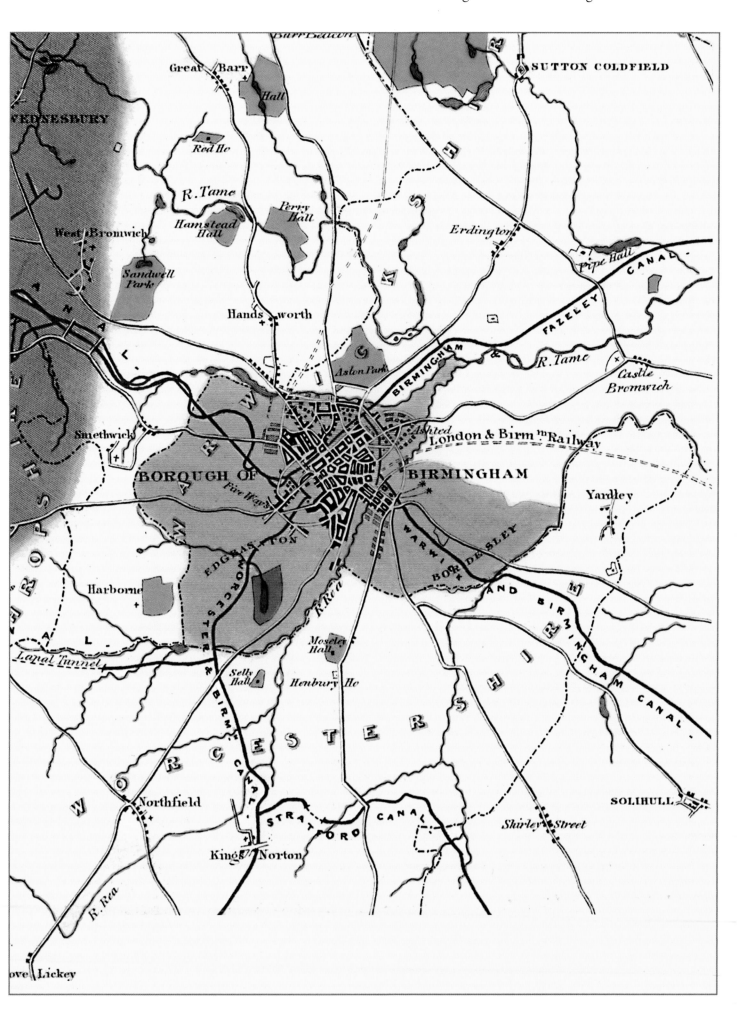

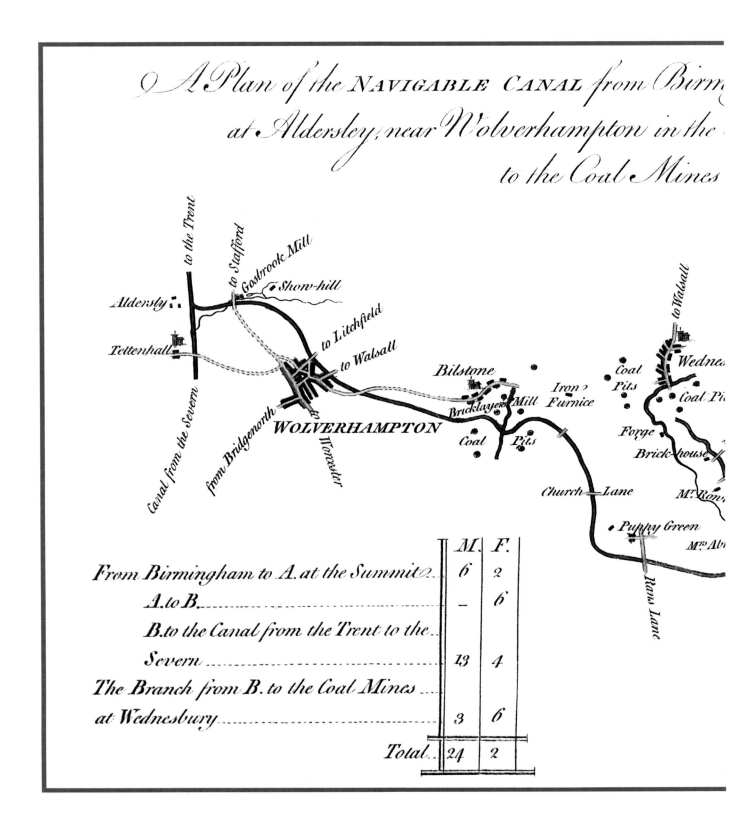

A Plan of the NAVIGABLE CANAL *from Birm...*
at Aldersley, near Wolverhampton in the...
to the Coal Mines...

	M.	F.
From Birmingham to A. at the Summit	6	2
A. to B.	–	6
B. to the Canal from the Trent to the Severn	13	4
The Branch from B. to the Coal Mines at Wednesbury	3	6
Total	24	2

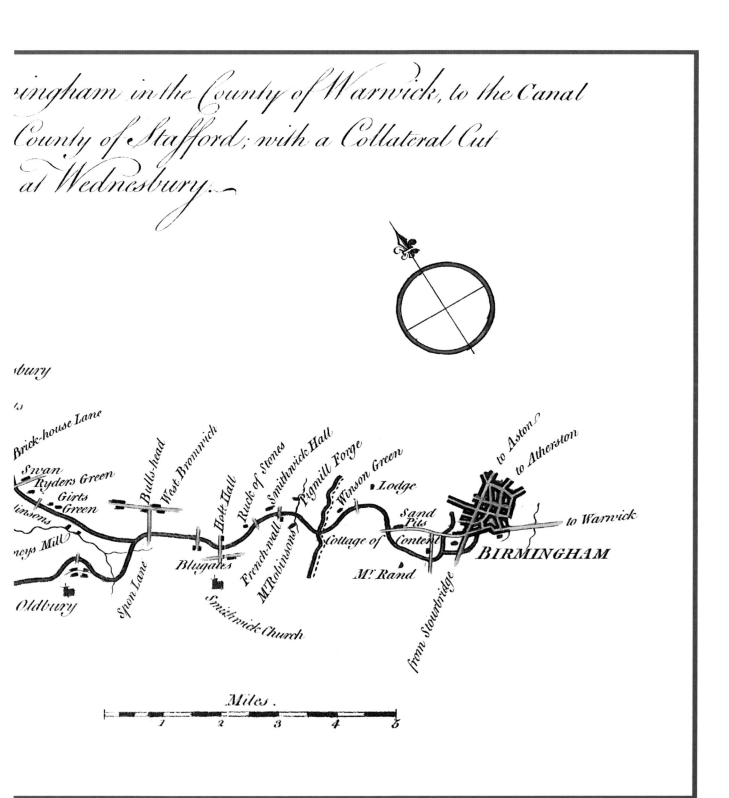

ringham in the County of Warwick, to the Canal

County of Stafford; with a Collateral Cut

at Wednesbury.

bury

Brick-house Lane

Swan

Ryders Green

Girts Green

insons

neys Mill

Oldbury

Bulls-head

Spon Lane

West Bromwich

Holt Hall

Blugates

Smithwick Church

Ruck of Stones

Smithwick Hall

French-wall

M.ʳ Robinsons

Pigmill Forge

Cottage of Content

Winson Green

Lodge

Sand Pits

M.ʳ Rand

to Aston

to Atherston

BIRMINGHAM

to Warwick

from Stourbridge

Miles.

1   2   3   4   5

BIRMINGHAM CANAL NAVIGATIONS

In March 1768 work first started on the building of the canals that would link Birmingham's thriving industry with coal mines of the Black Country, as well as the Staffordshire and Worcester Canal via Tipton, Bilston and Smethwick. The stretch from the coal mines at Wednesbury to Paradise Street was in operation by the end of 1769: The latter stages of the project were not so brisk. The Birmingham canal terminus was reached at New Hall Street in 1771: a year later the connecting locks at Wolverhampton were completed, joining the canal with Staffordshire and Worcestershire.

The plan by John Hancox shows those portions of the mineral districts of South Staffordshire, East Worcestershire and North Warwickshire, intersected by the Birmingham Canal Navigations. Dated 1864 it shows the full extent of the canal system.

The Birmingham Canal Lock Gate
Poem by Ian Henery

We used to meet by the old lock gate
Along the canal, your smile in my heart.
I come here often now we are apart
And for you, by narrow boats, I will wait.
Hand in hand on towpaths we walked on dates
The canal, like a river, in the sun.
Straight as Cupid's arrow the horizon
But time changes all and this is my fate.

Canal stretches forward across the land
And narrow boats pass through the locks and go;
Water is a constant, it has no flow,
Just like when you gave me your heart and hand.
All seasons change, nothing lasts forever,
Here I remain; desert my post? Never!
My heart at attention, yours to command.

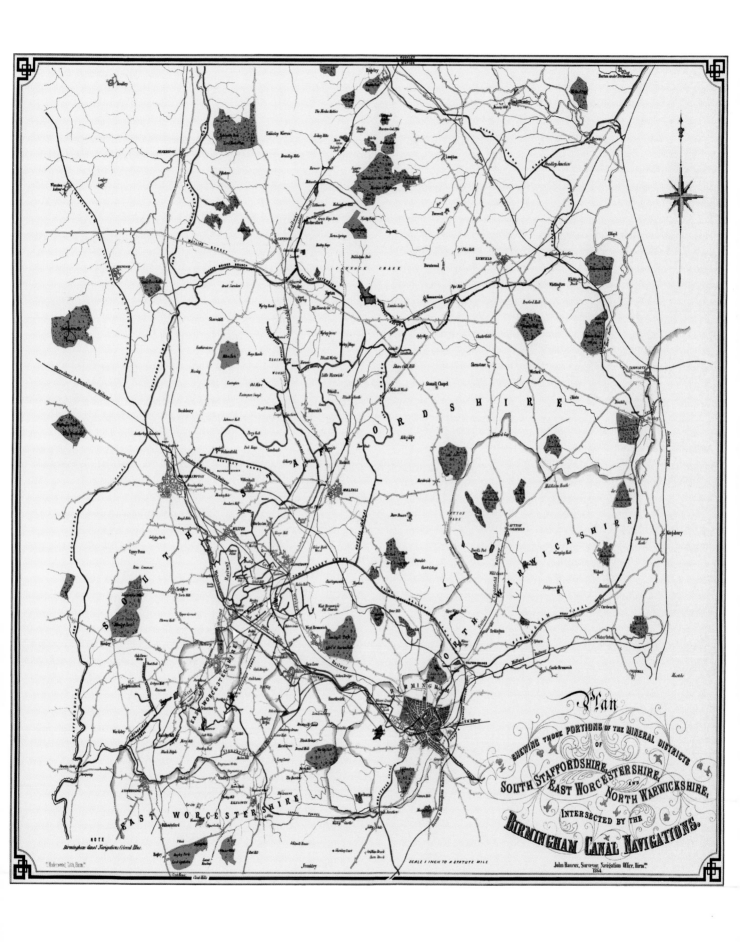

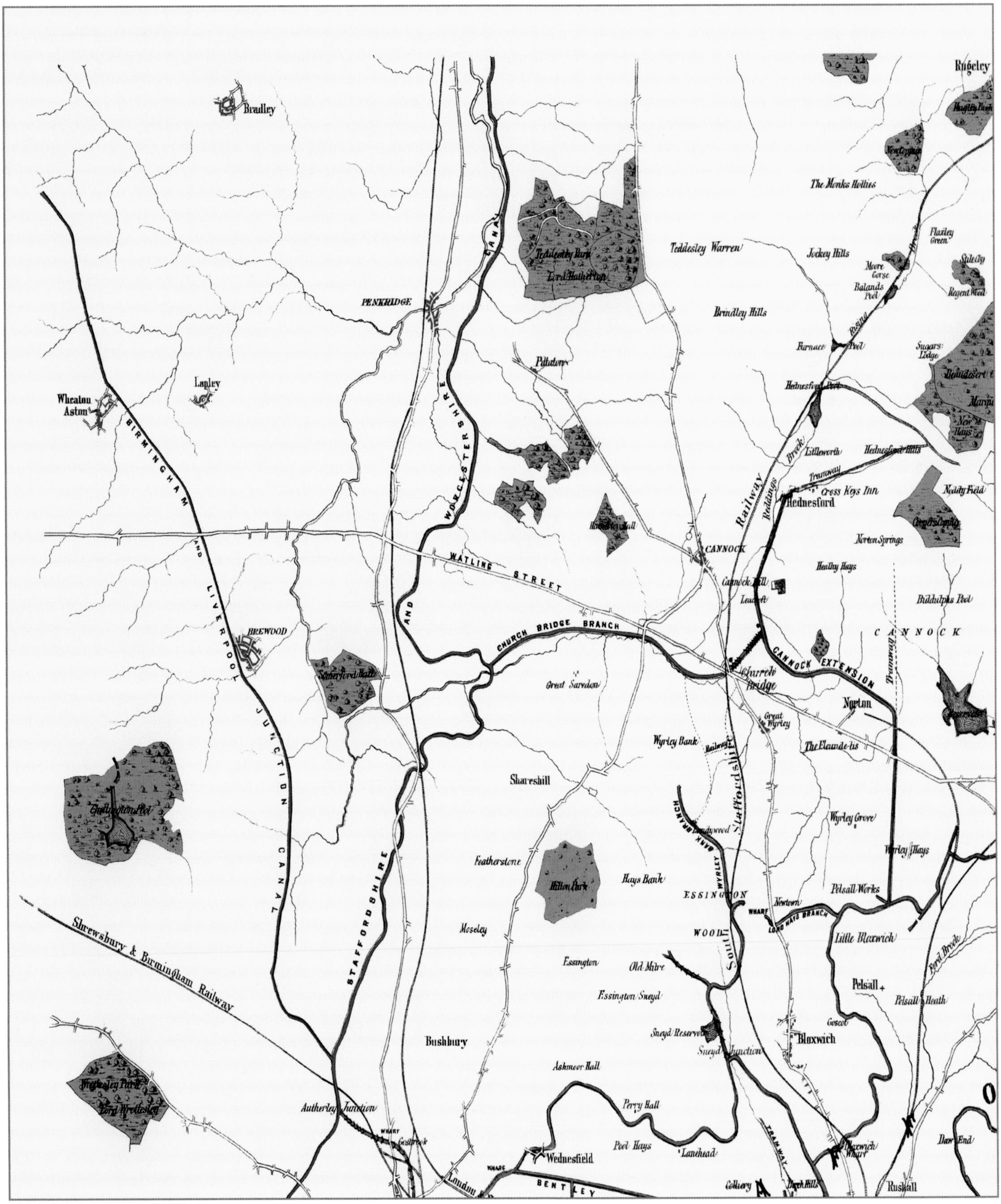
Bradley
Rugeley
Teddesley Park
Lord Hatherton
PENKRIDGE
CANAL
Teddesley Warren
The Monks Hollies
Jockey Hills
Brindley Hills
Whealon Aston
Lapley
Pillaton
Furnace
Pool
Hednesford Pool
Sugars Lodge
Beaudesert
Littleworth
Hednesford Hills
Tramway
Cross Keys Inn
Hednesford
Railway
Norton Springs
BIRMINGHAM AND LIVERPOOL JUNCTION CANAL
WORCESTERSHIRE
STAFFORDSHIRE AND WORCESTERSHIRE
WATLING STREET
CANNOCK
Healthy Hays
Leacroft
BREWOOD
CHURCH BRIDGE BRANCH
Church Bridge
CANNOCK EXTENSION
Great Saredon
Norton
Great Wyrley
Wyrley Bank
The Fleurde-lis
Shareshill
South Staffordshire
WYRLEY BANK BRANCH
Landywood
Wyrley Grove
Wyrley Hays
Featherstone
Hilton Park
Hays Bank
ESSINGTON WOOD
WHARF
LORD HAYS BRANCH
Newtown
Pelsall Works
Moseley
Little Bloxwich
Shrewsbury & Birmingham Railway
STAFFORDSHIRE
Essington
Old Mitre
Essington Sneyd
Pelsall
Pelsall Heath
Sneyd Reservoir
Sneyd Junction
Goscot
Bloxwich
Bushbury
Ashmoor Hall
Perry Hall
Autherley Junction
Wednesfield
Poel Hays
Lanehead
TRAMWAY
Bloxwich Wharf
Daw End
London
BENTLEY
Colliery
Rushall
Biddulphs Pool
Moore Gorse
Balands Pool
Flaxley Green
Regent Wood
New Hays
Neddy Field

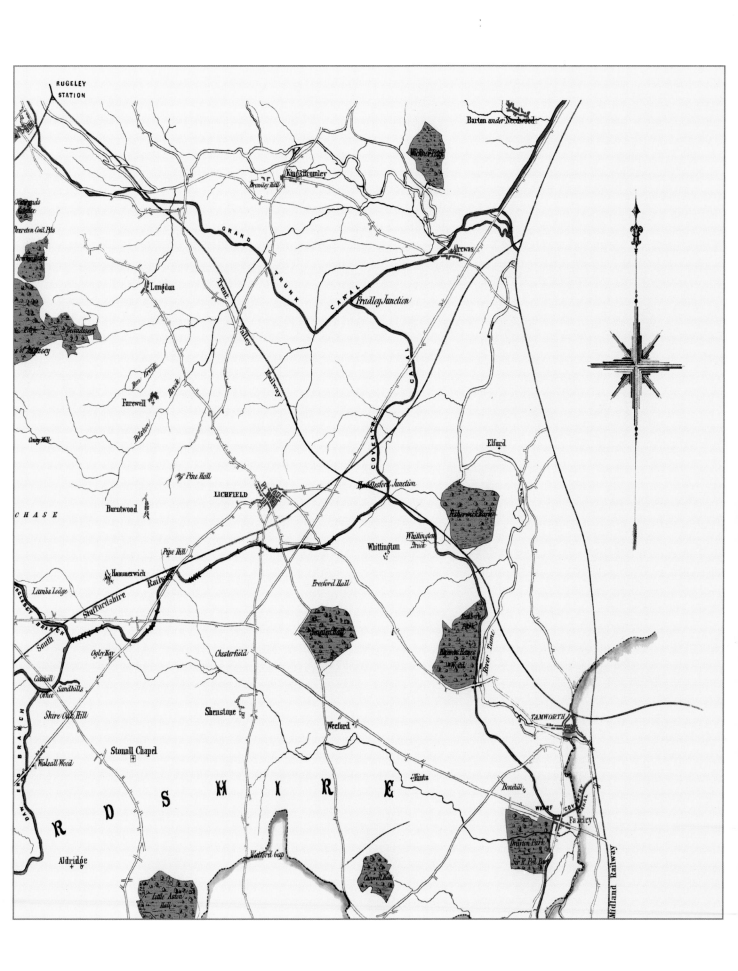

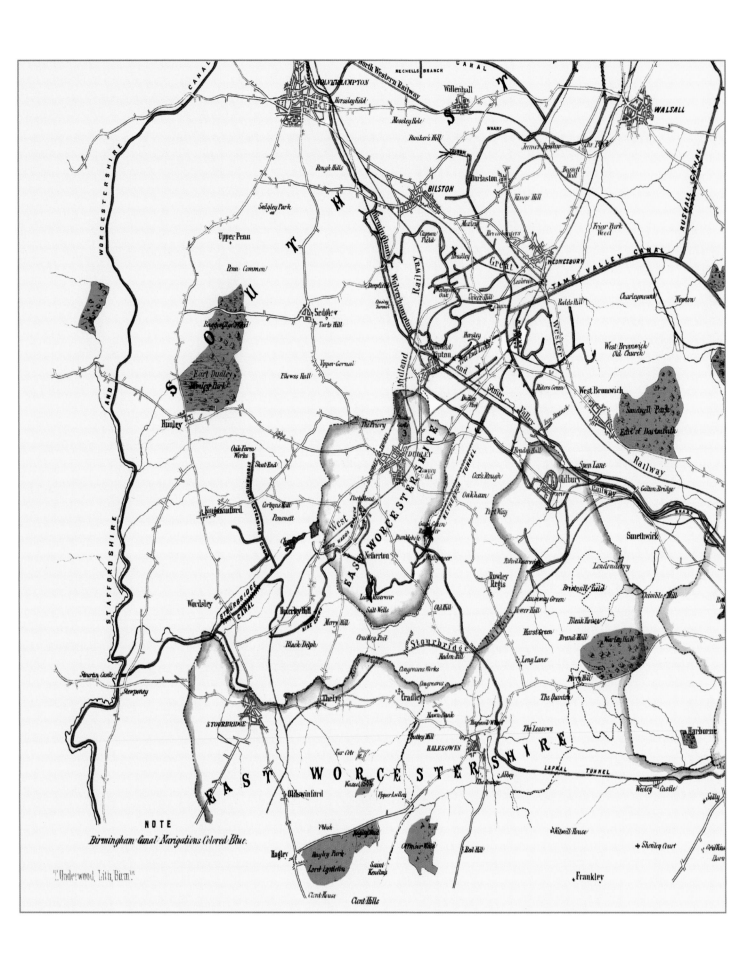

NOTE

Birmingham Canal Navigations Colored Blue.

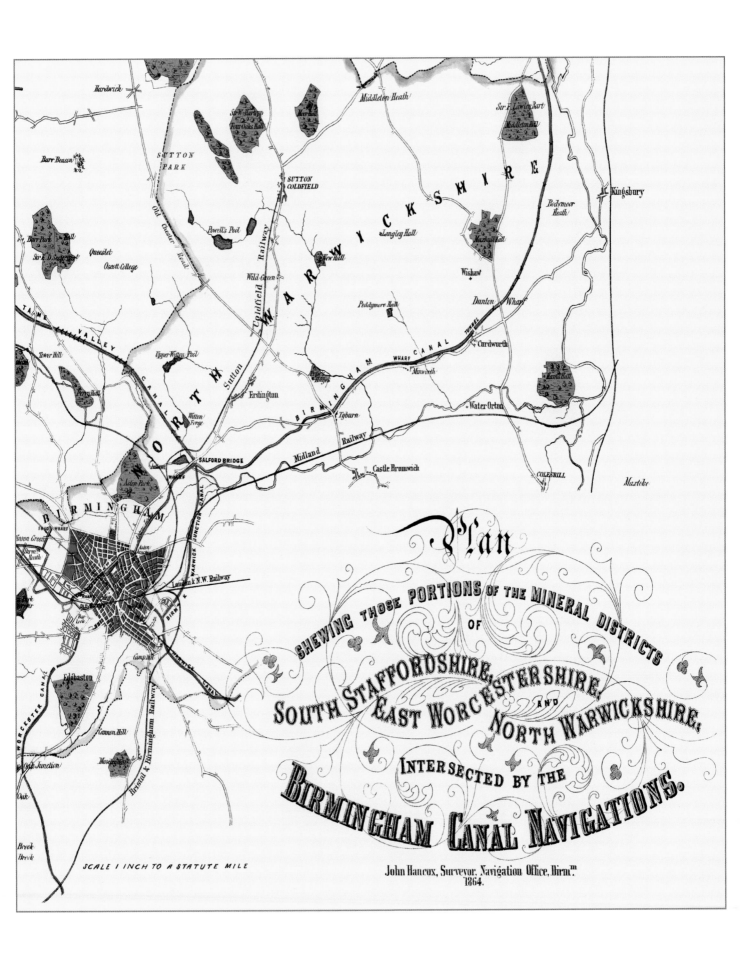

SCALE 1 INCH TO A STATUTE MILE

Plan

SHEWING THOSE PORTIONS OF THE MINERAL DISTRICTS

OF

SOUTH STAFFORDSHIRE, EAST WORCESTERSHIRE, AND NORTH WARWICKSHIRE,

INTERSECTED BY THE

BIRMINGHAM CANAL NAVIGATIONS.

John Hancox, Surveyor, Navigation Office, Birmm.
1864.

THE BUILDINGS OF BIRMINGHAM

PAST AND PRESENT

VOLUME TWO 1869

In concluding his description of the sketches in volume 1, Samuel Timmins indicated his desire to acquire further sketches of other old buildings in our town. These were sub-sequently obtained and three years later the second volume was published. This volume contained no introductory account, simply the many sketches that now follow.

A History in Buildings
Poem by Ian Henery

The remains of Herculaneum and Pompeii
Are remarkable for what they portray.
Two towns captured and frozen in time,
Embalmed human beings performing a mime.
The towns preserved for all posterity,
Ageless in their dark curiosity.

Towns are living, breathing organisms,
Colours shining through them like a prism.
Towns evolve and like a snake sheds its skin,
Allowing us to see its heart within.
They are a heaving, dynamic mass
And home to people from all types of class.

A rainbow of colours, different shades,
Reflecting lives and cultures we have made,
Forever changing, it does not stand still.
Recorded in buildings, not on handbills,
Buildings tell a story that we can see,
Coaxed into life by archaeology.

Much has been lost and not drawn or engraved,
No recordings kept and nothing has been saved.
The past matters as financial concerns;
Stories need to be told and lessons learned.
All old buildings should have plans in archives
For these old bricks outlast our human lives.

Birmingham's buildings, a forgotten mine,
Local legacies are bright stars that shine.
Buildings are epitaphs to those now lost
And must be preserved in art at all cost.
Buildings are like roots in our nation's soul,
The preservation of which is a goal.

VIEW OF HIGH ST. BIRMINGHAM - 1812

PRINTING OFFICE

HEN & CHICKEN HOTEL, NEW ST. - 1830

CASTLE INN, HIGH ST. - 1830

ROYAL HOTEL BIRMINGHAM, WILDAY & Co. - 1830

NELSON HOTEL LATER THE DOG INN - 1830

MESS'RS WHATELEY'S PREMISES BENNETT'S HILL - 1830

OLD HOUSES IN HIGH ST. - 1830

T. WESTON

GLOVER HOSIER AND HABERDASHER.

WHALEBONE CANE
WHOLESALE & RETAIL.

IMPORTER OF
FOREIGN.
BEADS TOYS &c

CONGREVE ST. & ANN ST. - 1869

OLD HOUSES, MOOR ST. - 1866

ST. MARTIN'S LANE - 1840

SWAN

SWA... TWO NECKS

OLD BUILDINGS IN DIGBETH - 1869

LEATHERN BOTTLE, DIGBETH - c1830

THE WHITE LION, DIGBETH - 1835

GOOD ACCOMADATION FOR TRAVALLERS

STABLING

PRESBYTERIAN MEETING HOUSE - 1869

HOUSES IN EDGBASTON ST. - 1869

DUDLEY ST. CORNER OF OLD MEETING ST. - 1869.

THE MALT SHOVEL INN, SMALLBROOK ST. - 1869

MALT SHOVEL INN

WINE & SPIRIT VAULTS

HARCOURT

THE CULLET, LICHFIELD ST. CORNER OF STAFFORD ST. - c1830

CORNER OF ASTON ST. & LANCASTER ST. – 1830

BIRMINGHAM STAGE-COACH,

In Two *Days* and a half; begins *May* the 24th, 1731.

SETS out from the *Swan-Inn* in *Birmingham*, every *Monday* at six a Clock in the Morning, through *Warwick*, *Banbury* and *Alesbury*, to the *Red Lion Inn* in *Aldersgate street*, *London*, every *Wednesday* Morning: And returns from the said *Red Lion Inn* every *Thursday* Morning at five a Clock the same Way to the *Swan-Inn* in *Birmingham* every *Saturday*, at 21 Shillings each Passenger, and 18 Shillings from *Warwick*, who has liberty to carry 14 Pounds in Weight, and all above to *pay One Penny a Pound*.
Perform d (if God permit)

By Nicholas Rothwell.

The Weekly Waggon sets out every *Tuesday from the Nagg s-Head in Birmingham. to the* Red Lion Inn *aforesaid, every Saturday, and returns from the said Inn every Monday, to the Nagg's-Head in Lirmingham every Thursday.*

Note. *By the* said Nicholas Rothwell at Warwick, *all Persons may be furnished with a By-Coach, Chariot. Chaise, or Hearse, with a Mourning Coach and able Horses, to any Part of Great Britain, at reasonable Rates : And also Saddle Horses to be had.*

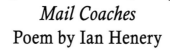

Mail Coaches
Poem by Ian Henery

The full moon was a ghostly galleon,
Night wind was an ocean in the tall trees;
Cries of owls were surf on rocks in the breeze,
Our mail coach pulled by four black stallions
Flying across the face of Albion.
Bridles twinkled, twinkled in the starlight,
Heading for Birmingham and the daylight,
Speedy communication championed.

We float like a phantom across the miles,
Drum of horses` hooves on the dusty road;
We have Birmingham`s mail, a precious load,
Delivered before the sun kisses tiles,
Past sleeping villages, hedgerows and stiles.
Waiting, waiting for us are the stables,
A hot bath and feast at tavern tables,
Birmingham`s coach house and my sweetheart`s smile.

Our mail coach unites us all by design:
Companies, friends and parents by letters,
Our new age miracle is unfettered.
Birmingham, a warm bed and glass of wine,
Dry stables and tavern where I can dine.
Its dawning, dawning, end of our night ride,
The mail delivered and source of our pride,
The countdown is marked by the stone road signs.

PROSPECT VIEWS AND PERIOD TOWN PLANS

The three prospect views that follow are reduced copies, digitally re-mastered, of some most valuable engravings, showing the aspects of three sides of our town at the time when William Westley's plan of Birmingham 1731 was "surveyed". A fourth "Prospect" was apparently intended, but has not yet been found, and was probably never published.

Plan of Birmingham 1795 Surveyed by Charles Pye: Shows the moat around the Old Manor House and the moat around the Parsonage. Interestingly he shows "The Crescent", a line of terraced houses built in a curve. The year this map was published only 12 out of 23 of the houses had been built mainly in the wings, due to lack of funding the grand scheme was never completed and it was eventually demolished.

Plan of Birmingham 1832, by James Drake: Shows around the edges, all of the streets, roads, avenues and places of worthy interest, with a unique grid layout allowing each entry to be quickly located on the plan. At the bottom, James Drake lists further fascinating information about Birmingham; this includes Post Office Regulations, Hackney Coach and Car Fares, Public Institutions, Stage Coaches, Inns and Wagon Warehouses.

Plan of Birmingham 1837, engraved by John Dower and published by William S. Orr: This detailed plan lists no fewer than 42 buildings in the reference table. The plan shows the proposed route into Birmingham of the Grand Junction Railway, with a terminus off Pritchett Street, Aston, presumably with an end link with the London line at Curzon Street. The SDUK map published later in 1839 illustrates the actual completed and opened routes into Birmingham.

Plan of Birmingham, 1839, from the Society for the Diffusion of Useful Knowledge (SDUK): Founded in 1827 by John Earl Russell and Henry Brougham, later Chancellor of England. Their greatest publication was their atlas of the world, entitled "Maps of the Society for the Diffusion of Useful Knowledge". The fine steel engravings are hand–coloured and often embellished with vignettes and comparisons of the height of the principal buildings of the town or city, as with the Birmingham plan of 1839.

THE NORTH PROSPECT OF ST. PHILIPS CHURCH, &C. IN BIRMINGHAM.

1 St Philips Church Designd by
Tho.s Archer Esq.r in y.e year 1710.
2 A new Charity School wherein are Cloathed
taught & maintained upwards of 80 Boys & Girls.

To the R.t Hon.ble William Lord Digby, Andrew Archer, and
Thomas Archer, Esq.rs the Surviving Trustees for building S.t Philips Church
this Plate is humbly Dedicated by their most obedient humble Serv.t W. Westley.

3 The Rectors house.
4 Temple Row.
5 S.t Martins Church.
6 &c. New Hall Road.

103

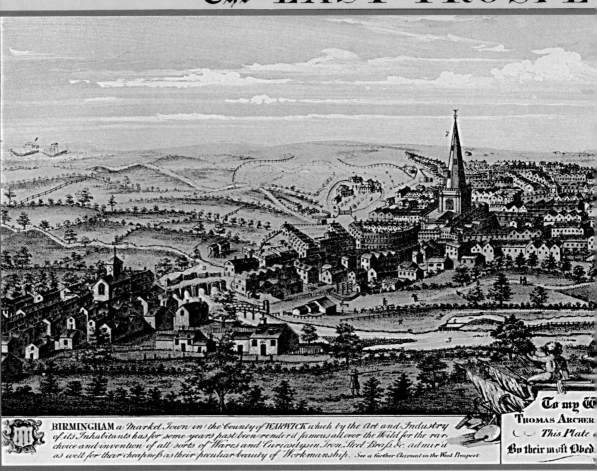

BIRMINGHAM a Market Town in the County of WARWICK which by the Art and Industry of its Inhabitants has for some years past been render'd famous all over the World for the rare choice and invention of all sorts of Wares and Curiositys in Iron, Steel, Brass &c. admir'd as well for their cheapness as their peculiar beauty of Workmanship. See a further Account in the West Prospect.

To my ☞
THOMAS ARCHER
This Plate
By their most Obed

THE SOUTH WEST PROSPECT OF BIR

BIRMINGHAM (anciently written BIRMYNCHAM als BRYMYNCHAM) is neither Borough nor C
& Ingenuity of its Inhabitants & the Advantage of its being an open, free place of Trade, it is become fam
a Competition with any of the most flourishing Towns in England; being adorn'd with several beautiful S
Girls, and a Free Grammar School, founded and endow'd with a large revenue by King Edward the sixt
weekly market on Thursday, with two Annual Fairs; one on Ascension day & the other on the feast of St.
House. 6. The Parsonage House. 7. Charbury Forrest in Leicester Shire. 8 St. Martin's Church. 9. Curdw
Chappel in Deretend. 17 Coleshall. 18. Yardeley.

1 Edgbaston the seat of Sr Henry Gough, Bar^t	4 the Antient Seat of the Lord Birmingham	7 St Martin's Church	10 St Philips Church	14 Presbyterian M^g H^{se}
2 St John's Chap^l in Deritend	5 the Lady's Well	8 the Old Crofs	11 New Hall	15 Baptifts Meet^g H^{se}
3 the River Rea	6 the Old Bath	9 a Free School founded by Edward y^e Sixth	12 the Square	16 the Old Mill House
			13 Welch Crofs	17 Cooper's Mill & H^{se}

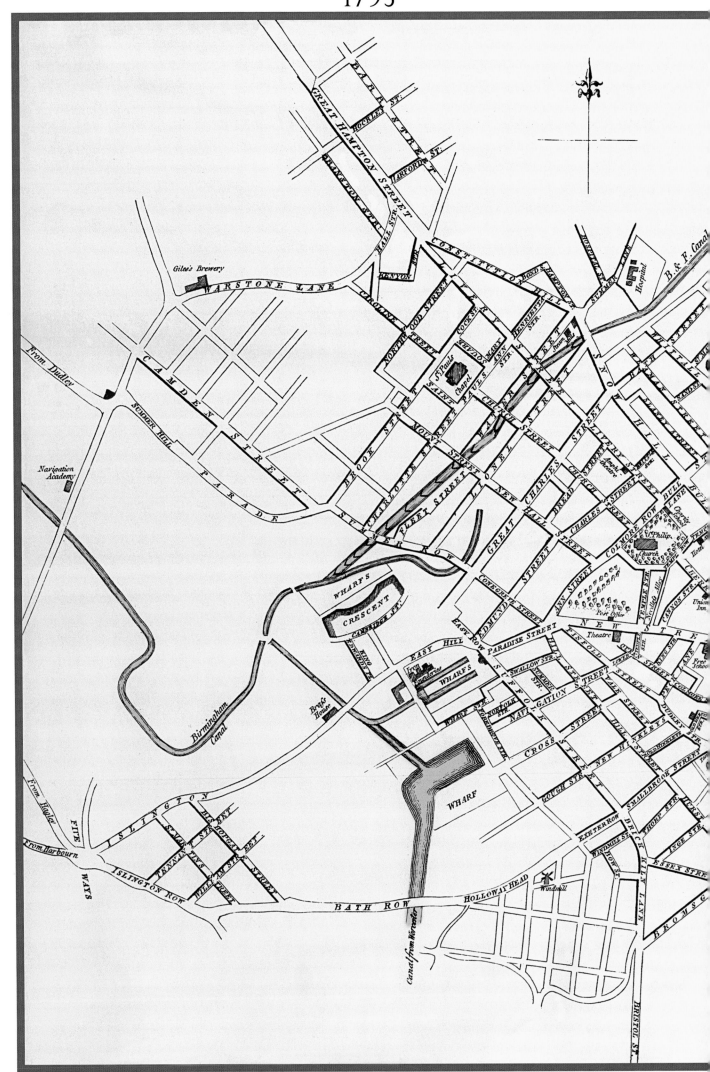

PLAN OF BIRMINGHAM, SURVEYED BY CHARLES PYE 1795

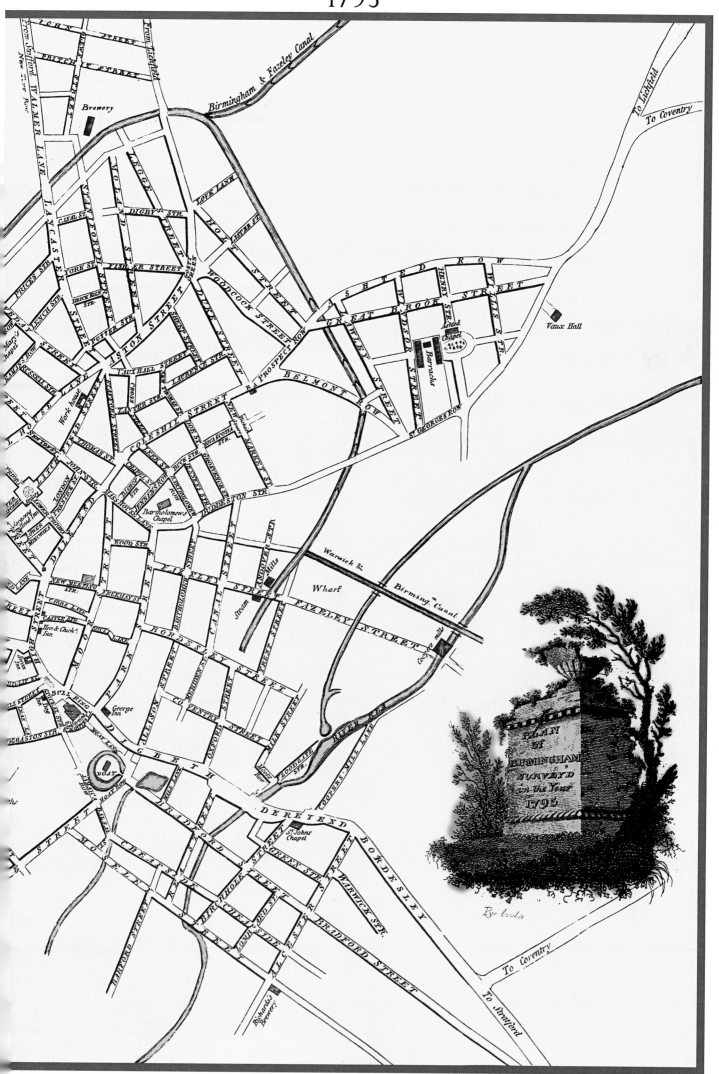

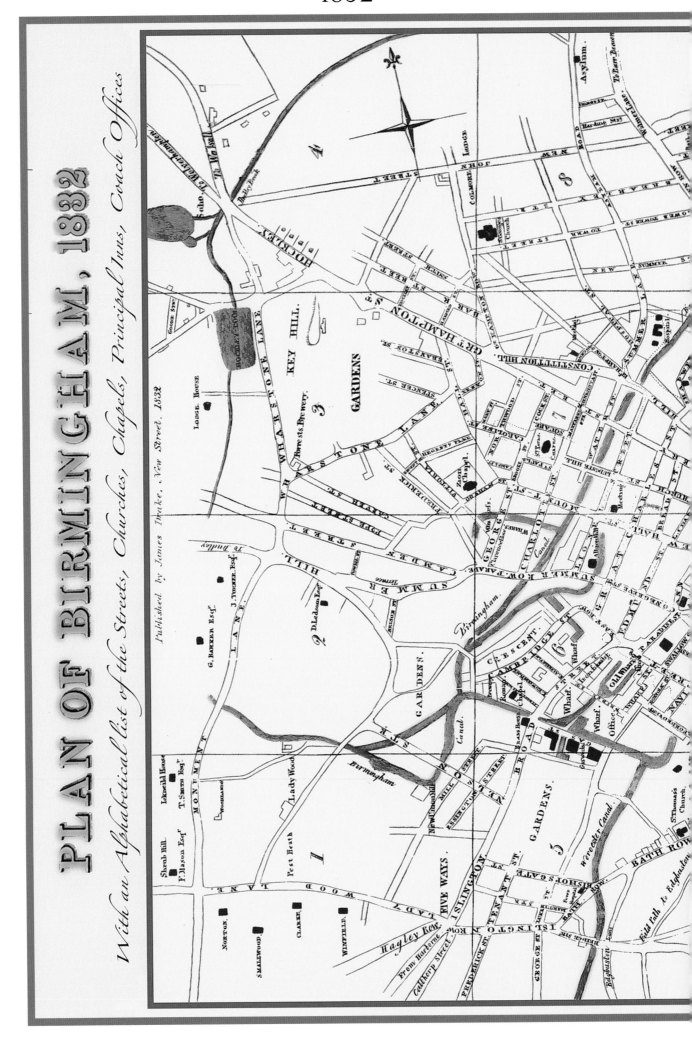

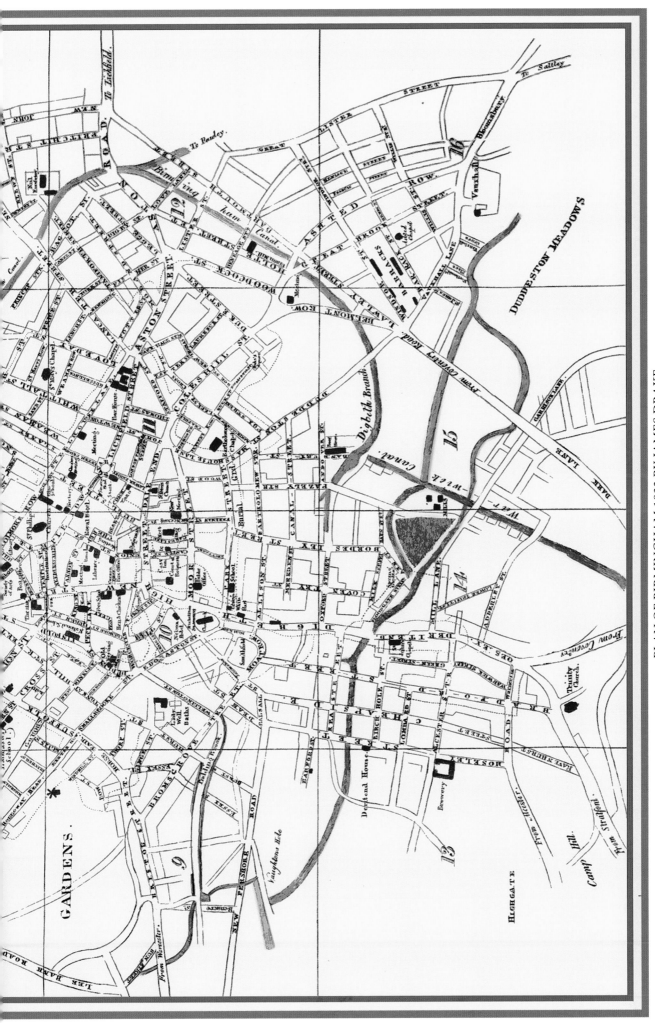

PLAN OF BIRMINGHAM 1832 BY JAMES DRAKE

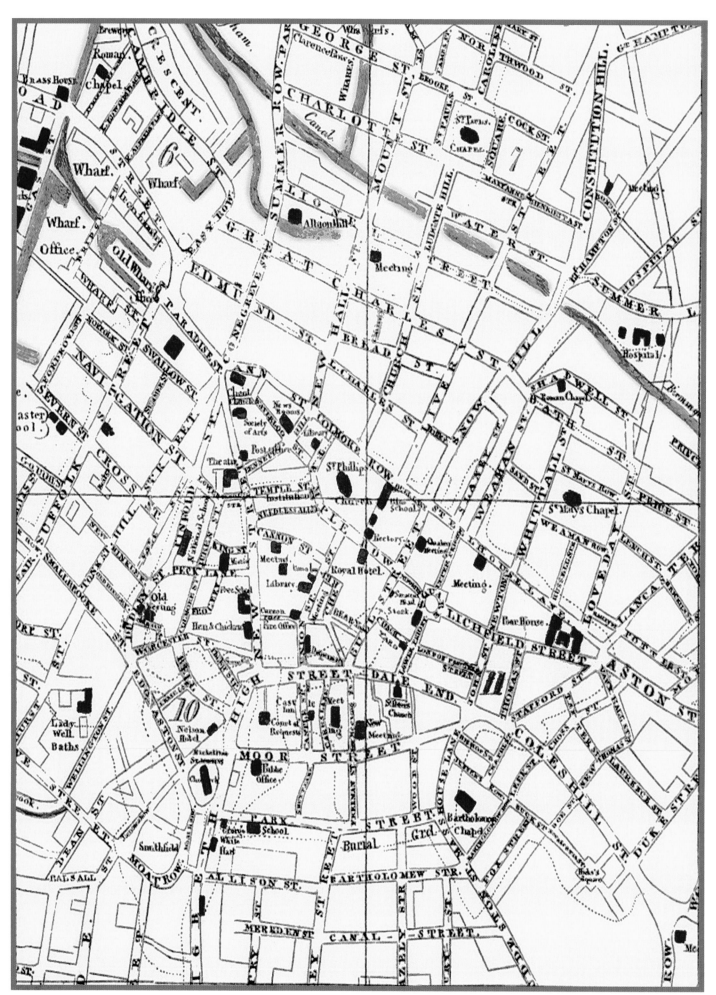

Plan of Birmingham 1832 (Centre segment).

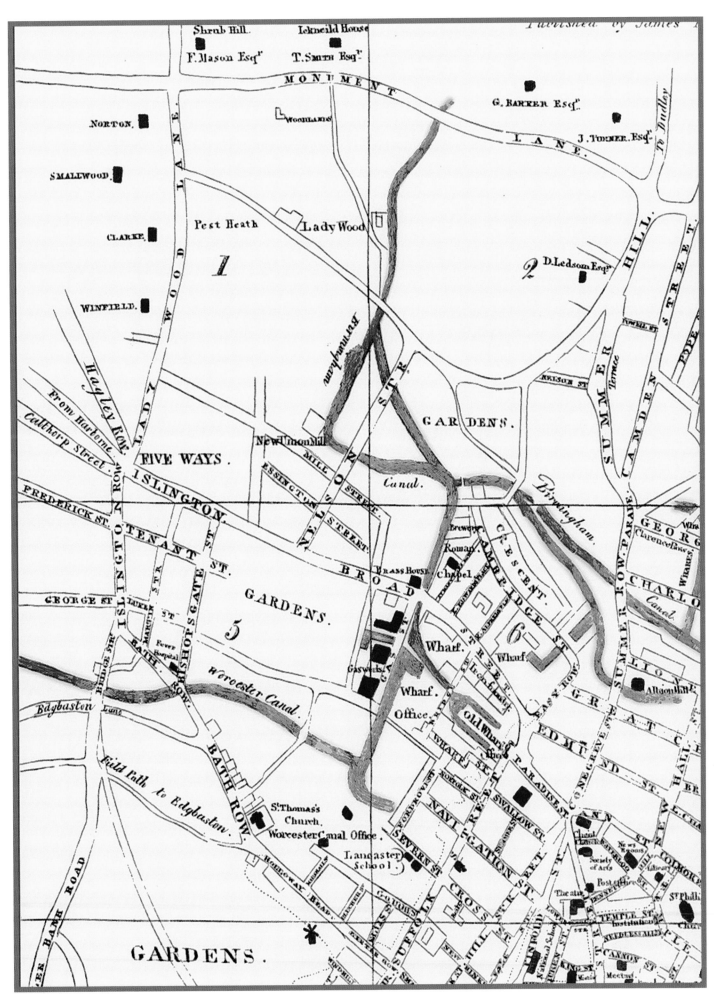

Plan of Birmingham 1832 (Top left segment).

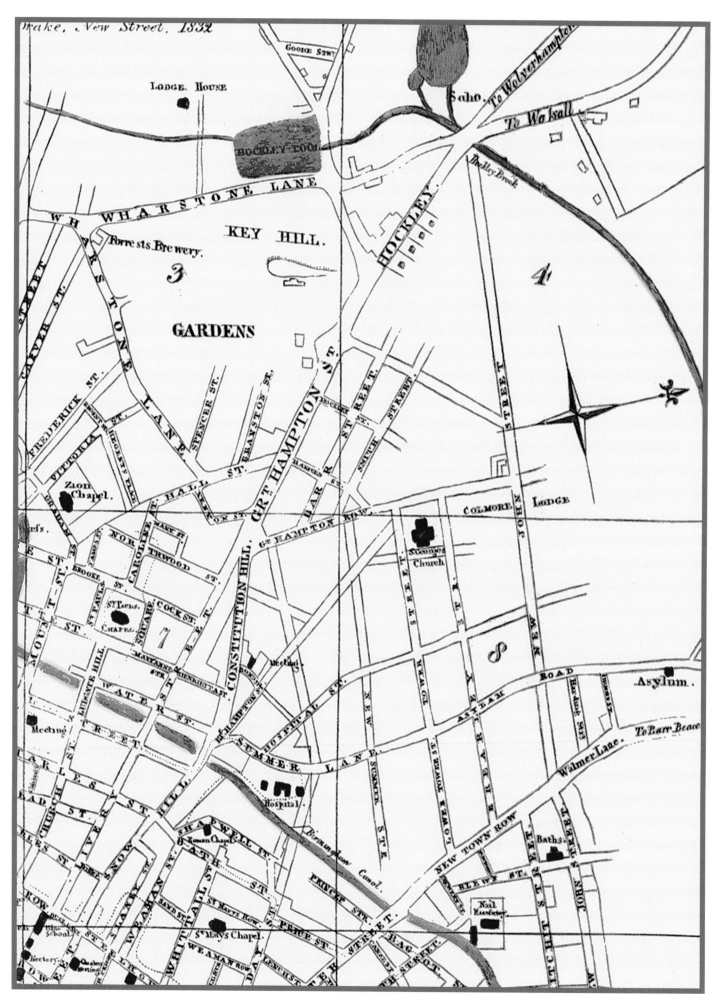

Plan of Birmingham 1832 (Top right segment).

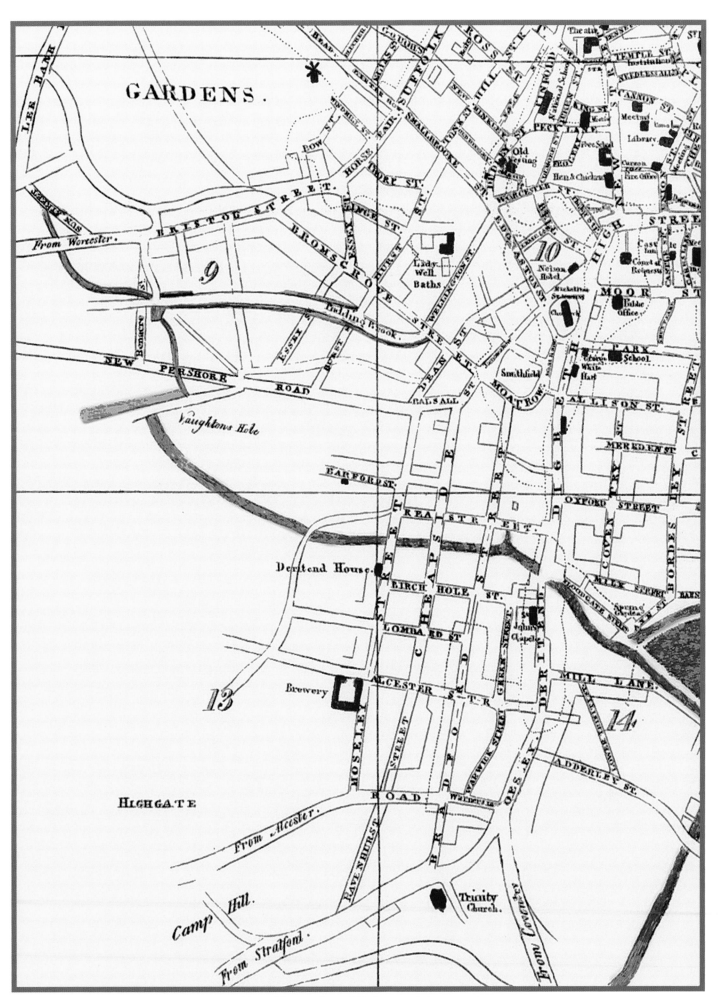

Plan of Birmingham 1832 (Bottom left segment).

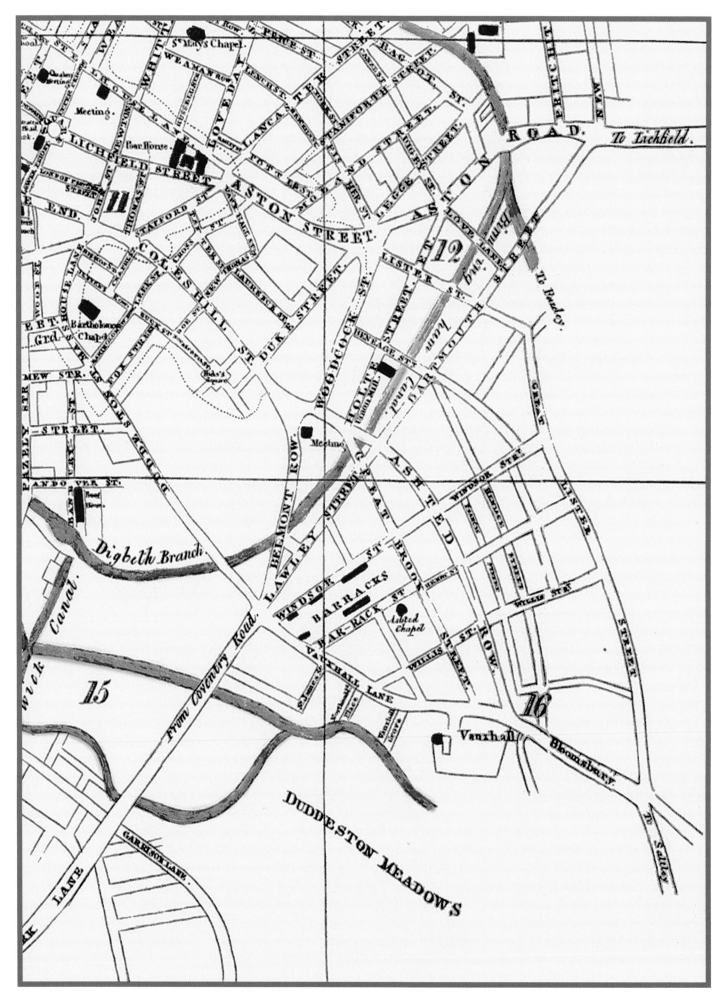

Plan of Birmingham 1832 (Bottom right segment).

INDEX

POST OFFICE REGULATIONS

Mails	Depart	Arrive	Letters ready at.
Manchester	45m. p.5 morn.	25m p 7 even.	¾ p.7
Liverpool[*]	8 even.	½ p.6 morn.	7
Sheffield	6 morn.	¼ 4 aftern.	½ p. 4
Stamford and Leicester	8 morn.	5 aftern.	6
Holyhead	5m. p. 8 morn.	5 aftern.	6
Walsall	10m. p. 8 morn.	¼ p.5aftern.	6
Kidderminster, Dudley, &c.	10m. p. 8 morn.	½ p.5 aftern.	6
Oxford	¾ p. 2 aftern.	11 morn.	½ p 11
London, via Warwick	¼ p. 5 aftern.	½ p. 9 morn.	10
London, via Coventry	50m. p. 5 aftern.	½ p. 7 morn.	¼ p. 8
Bristol	8 even.	5morn.	7

☞ The Office is shut at Eight o'clock in the morning.

Letters should be put in an hour before the departure of the several Mails: if after that time, one penny is paid to ensure their being forwarded.

* This mail also takes second bags for Manchester and neighbouring places.

HACKNEY COACH AND CAR FARES

CARRIAGES DRAWN BY TWO HORSES

	s.	d.
Any distance not exceeding ½ Mile	1	0
Exceeding ½ Mile, and not exceeding 1 Mile	1	6
———— 1 —————————— 1 ½ —	2	0
———— 1 ½ —————————— 2 —	2	6
———— 2 —————————— 3 —	3	6
———— 3 —————————— 4 —	5	0

CARS AND OTHER CARRIAGES DRAWN BY ONE HORSE

	s.	d.
Any distance not exceeding 1 Mile	1	0
Exceeding 1 Mile, and not exceeding 1 ½ Mile	1	6
———— 1 ½ —————————— 2 —	2	0
———— 2 —————————— 2 ½ —	2	6
———— 2 ½ —————————— 3 —	3	0
———— 3 —————————— 3 ½ —	3	6
———— 3 ½ —————————— 4 —	4	0

For returning, half the foregoing Fares; for waiting, 6d. for 20 minutes; and after twelve o'clock at night double Fares are charged.

PUBLIC INSTITUTIONS

Theatre, New Street	Free School, New Street
Society of Arts, New Street	Lady Well Baths, Hurst Street
Museum, Temple Row	Public Office, Moor Street
General Hospital, Summer Lane	Town Hall, Paradise Street
News Room, Bennett's Hill	Town Hall, New Street
Old Library, Union Street	Barracks, Great Brook Street
New Library, Temple	Proof House, Banbury Street
Row, West	Vauxhall
Workhouse, Lichfield Street	The Dispensary, Union Street
Court of Requests, High Street	Fever Hospital, Bath Row
Railway Office, Bennett's Hill	Magdalen Institution, Islington
Infant School, Ann Street	Savings Bank, Temple Row
Blue Coat School, St. Philip's	Philosophical Institution,
Church Yard	Cannon Street

Botanical and Horticultural Gardens, Edgbaston.

INNS

The Royal Hotel,	Temple Row ⎫
Radenhurst's, late	⎬ The Principal Family Houses.
Wilday's ditto	New Street ⎭
Stork,	Old Square, ⎫
Hen and Chickens,	New Street, ⎬ Family and Commercial.
Swan,	High Street and New Street, ⎭
Albion,	High Street, ⎫
Nelson,	High Street, ⎬
Castle,	High Street, ⎬ Coach, Family
Saracen's Head,	Bull Street, ⎬ and Commercial.
St. George's Tavern,	High Street, ⎭
Union,	Union Street, ⎫
White Hart,	Digbeth, ⎬
George,	Digbeth, ⎬ Chiefly
Woolpack,	Moor Street, ⎭ Commercial.

STAGE COACHES

At the Offices of any of the House specified in our List as COACH INNS, all information may be obtained as to the Departures of the several Stage and Mail Coaches.

THE PRINCIPAL WAGGON WAREHOUSE ARE,

For London, Oxford, Warwick, South-ampton, &c	Golby, 52, Dale-end, Jolly, Bromsgrove Street.
Bristol, Bath, Glocester, Worcester, Hereford, Sheffield, Derby, Notting-ham, Leicester, Cambridge, Liverpool, Manchester	Ashmore, Edgbaston Street, Wheatcroft, Crescent Wharf.
Bristol, Bath, Leicester	Howes & Co. Bordesley St.
Newcastle-on-Tyne, Cambridge, Liverpool, Manchester ⎫	Shackwell, Dale End.
⎬	Tombs, Bear Yard.
Shrewsbury and Wolverhampton ⎭	Wallis, 138 Moor Street.

Sundry minor Carriers at the Fountain, New Street; Barrel, Snow Hill; Rose, Edgbaston Street; Spread Eagle, Spiceal Street; Horeshoe, St. Martin's Lane; Bell, Phillip Street, &c.

The principal Wharf for the Conveyance of Goods by Canal are those near the Waterfront in Great Charles street: Danks and Co., Brown and Son, and Greaves in Broad Street; Swains, Friday bridge; Pickfords, at the Warwick Junction, Corbets, Aston road- from almost every one of which, Boats are daily or frequently loading to all principal points.

The Figures in the Consulting Index refer to the Squares into which, for ready reference, the map is divided.

1837

PLAN OF BIRMINGHAM 1837, ENGRAVED BY JOHN DOWER AND PUBLISHED BY WILLIAM S. ORR.

1837

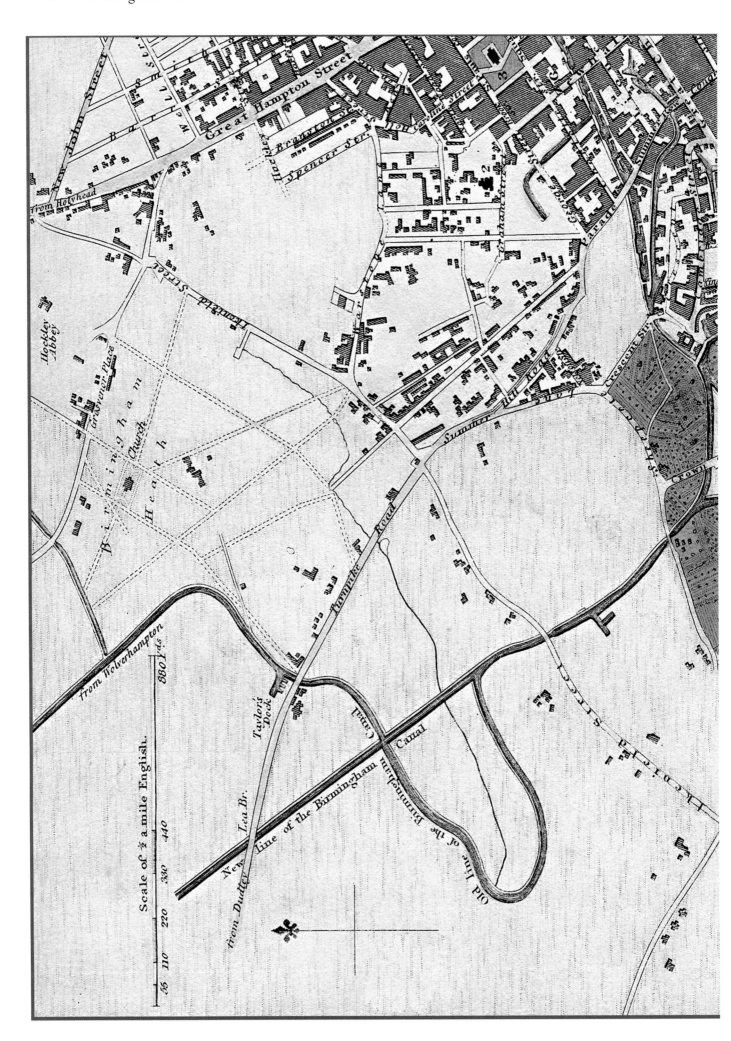

TOWN HALL.

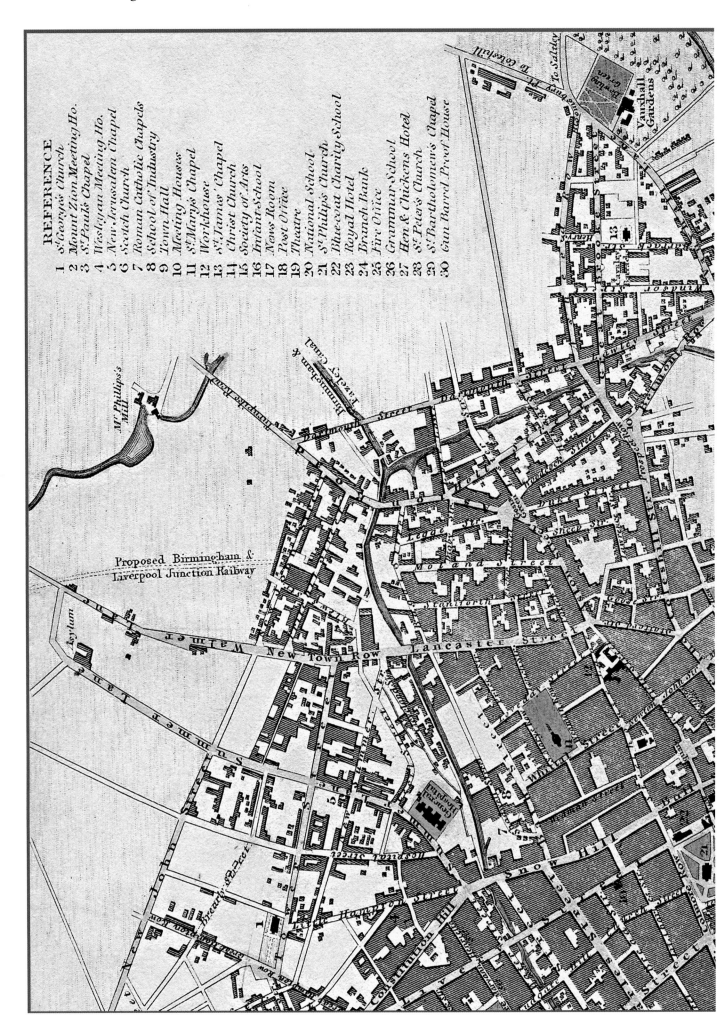

REFERENCE

1   St George's Church.
2   Mount Zion Meeting Ho.
3   St Paul's Chapel
4   Wesleyan Meeting Ho.
5   New Jerusalem Chapel
6   Scotch Church
7   Roman Catholic Chapels
8   School of Industry
9   Town Hall
10 Meeting House
11 St Mary's Chapel
12 Workhouse
13 St James' Chapel
14 Christ Church
15 Society of Arts
16 Infant School
17 News Room
18 Post Office
19 Theatre
20 National School
21 St Philip's Church
22 Blue-coat Charity School
23 Royal Hotel
24 Branch Bank
25 Fire Office
26 Grammar School
27 Hen & Chickens Hotel
28 St Peter's Church
29 St Bartholomew's Chapel
30 Gun Barrel Proof House

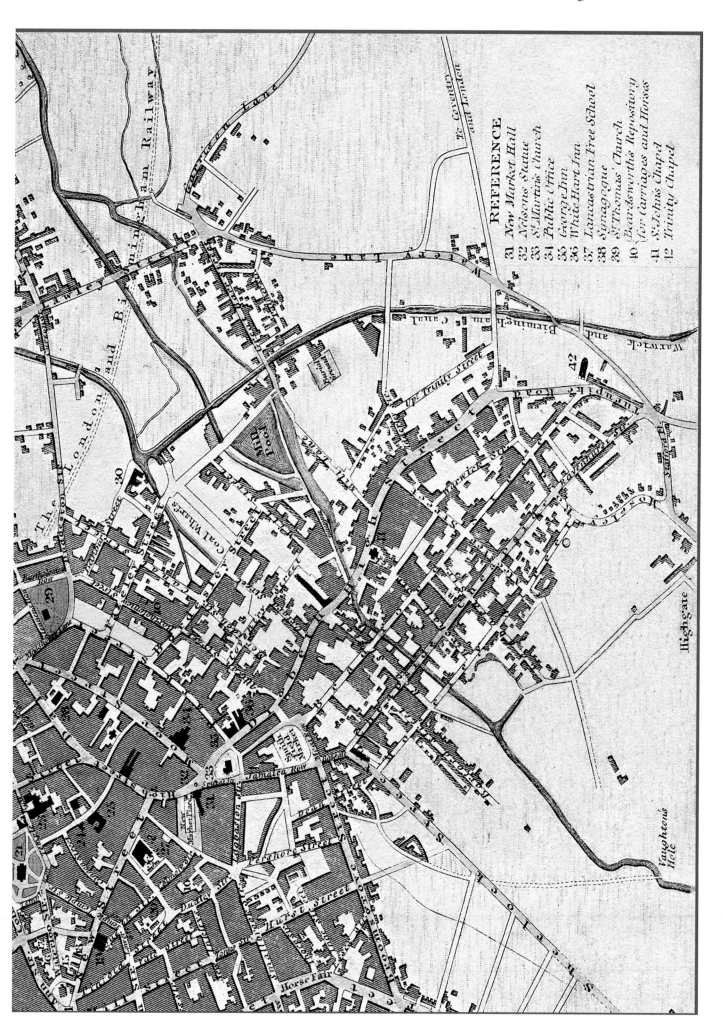

REFERENCE

31 New Market Hall
32 Nelson's Statue
33 St Martin's Church
34 Public Office
35 George Inn
36 White Hart Inn
37 Lancastrian Free School
38 Synagogue
39 St Thomas' Church
40 Beardsworth's Repository
    for carriages and Horses
41 St John's Chapel
42 Trinity Chapel

PLAN OF BIRMINGHAM, 1839, FROM THE SOCIETY FOR THE DIFFUSION OF USEFUL KNOWLEDGE (SD

PLAN OF BIRMINGHAM AND ITS ENVIRONS
(with the Boundaries taken from the Reform Act)

Scale of Miles

EXPLANATIONS.
Boundary of Borough
Boundaries of Parishes or Townsh.
Boundaries of Wards

REFERENCE TO THE WARDS

All Saints	1
Hockley	2
St Georges	3
St Martins	4
Duddeston and Nechels	5
Deritend and Bordesley	6
St Martins	7
St Thomas's	8
Lady Wood	9
Market Hall	10
St Peters	11
St Pauls	12
Edgbaston	13

London, Published by the Society for the Diffusion of Useful Knowledge, May 15th 1839.

Theatre Royal.   Free Grammar School

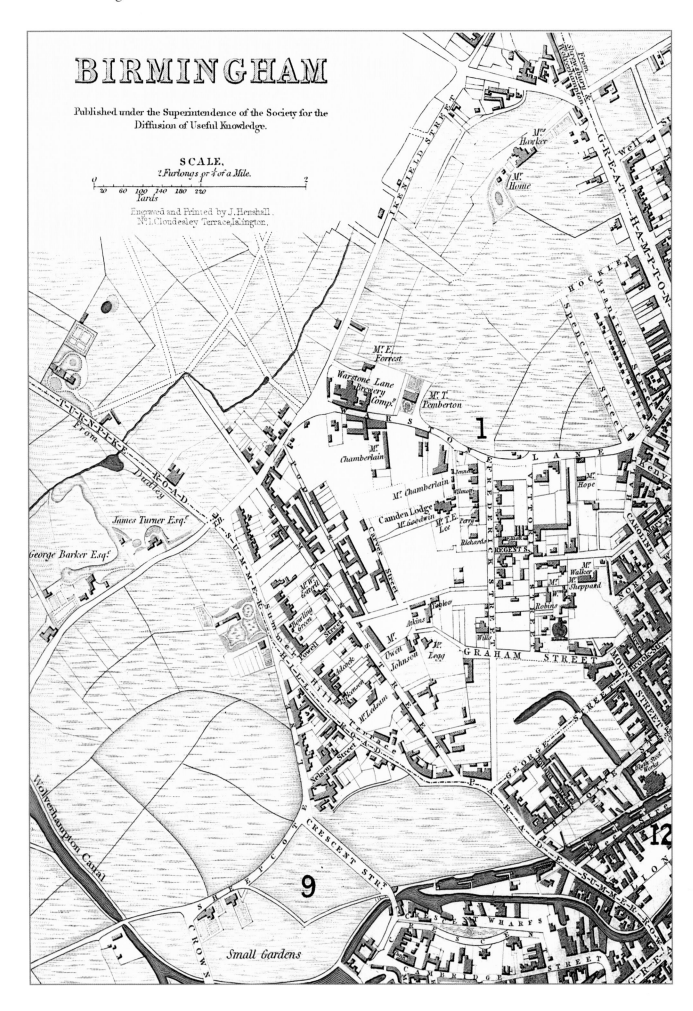

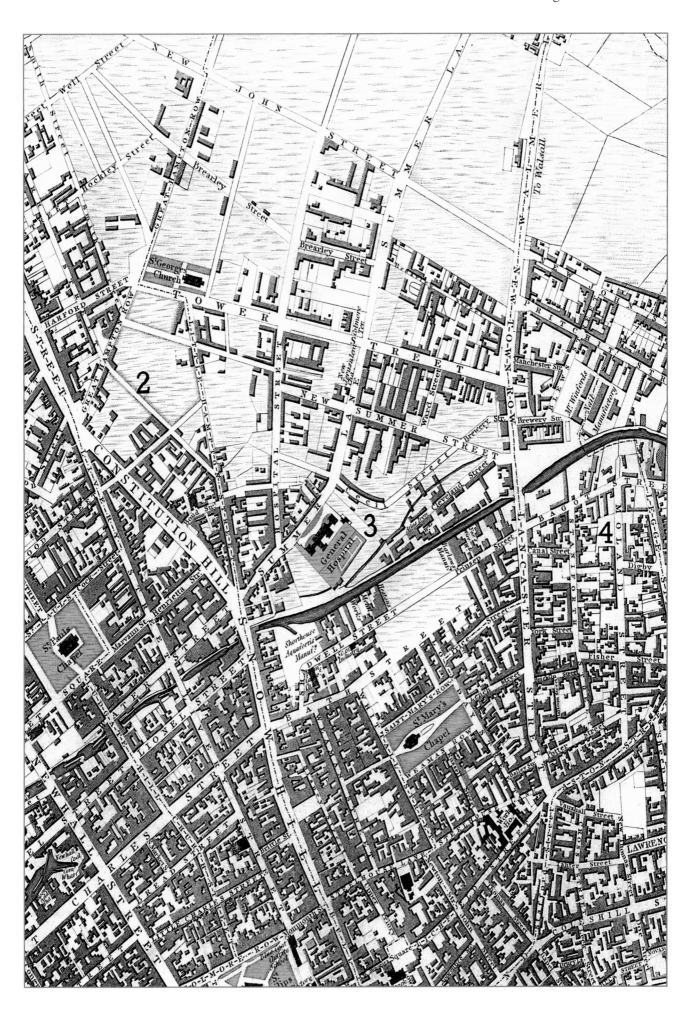

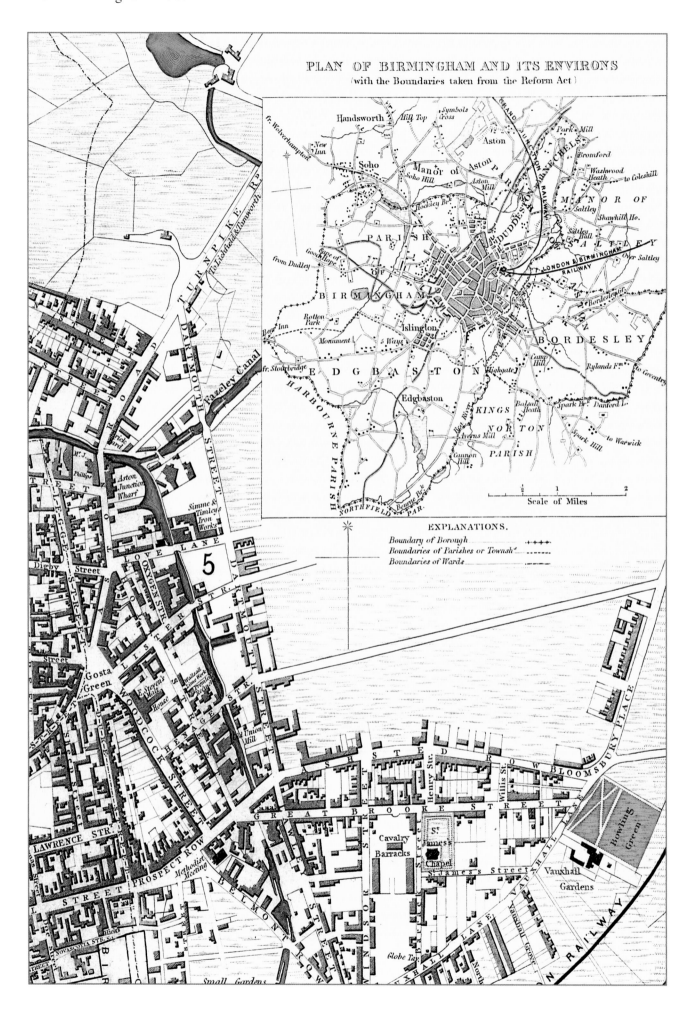

PLAN OF BIRMINGHAM AND ITS ENVIRONS
(with the Boundaries taken from the Reform Act)

EXPLANATIONS.

Boundary of Borough   +−+−+−+
Boundaries of Parishes or Townsh.ᵖ   − − − −
Boundaries of Wards

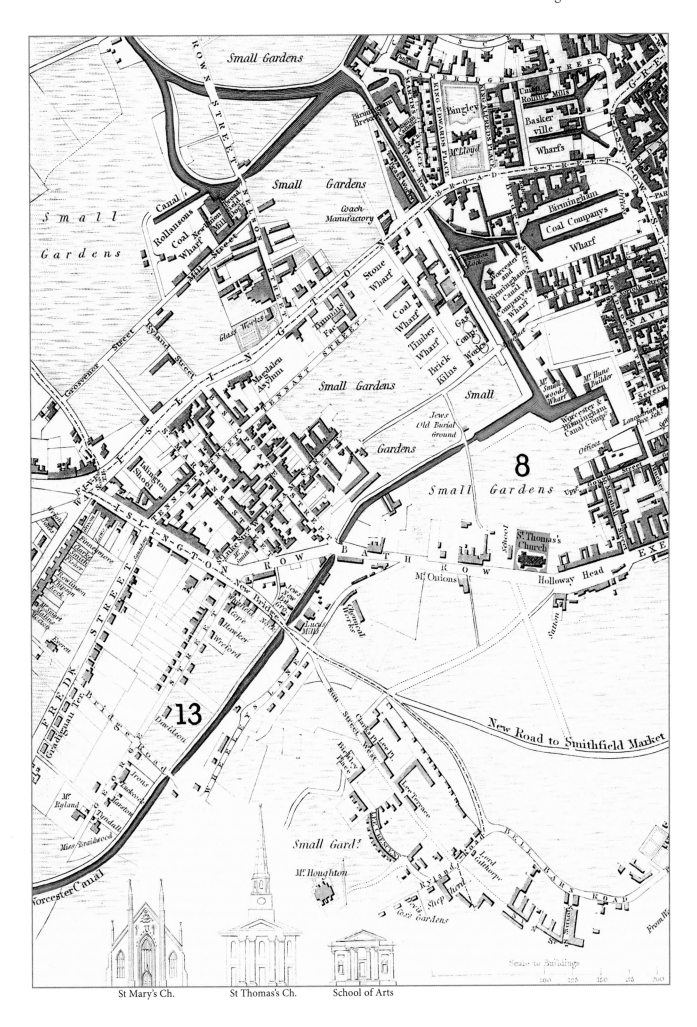

St Mary's Ch.   St Thomas's Ch.   School of Arts

Town Hall

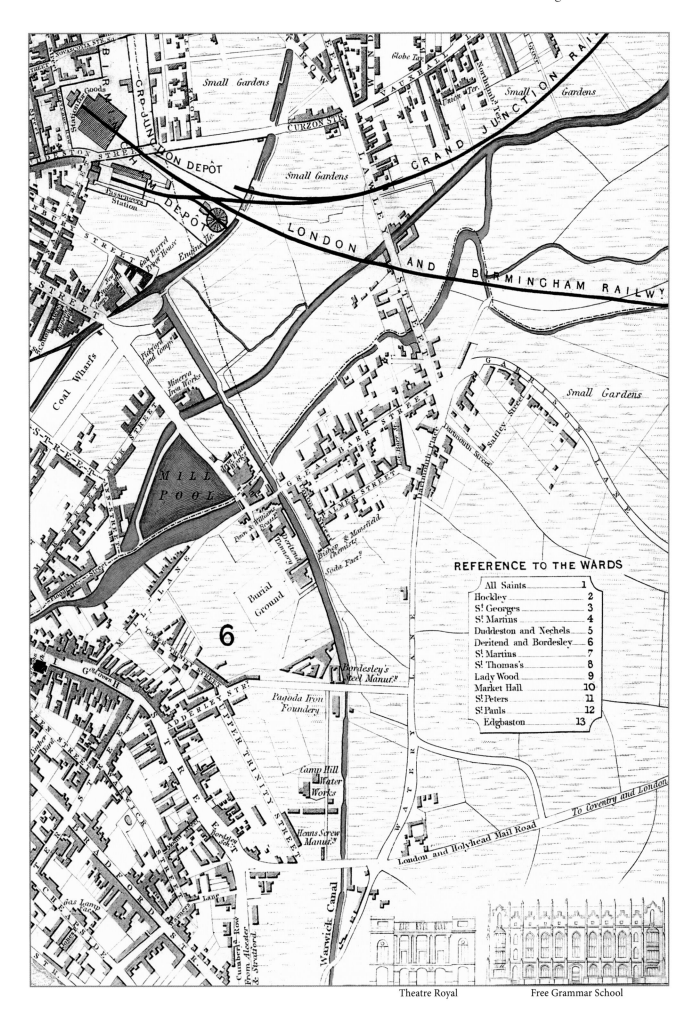

REFERENCE TO THE WARDS

All Saints	1
Hockley	2
St. Georges	3
St. Martins	4
Duddeston and Nechels	5
Deritend and Bordesley	6
St. Martins	7
St. Thomas's	8
Lady Wood	9
Market Hall	10
St. Peters	11
St. Pauls	12
Edgbaston	13

Theatre Royal   Free Grammar School

PICTURE CREDITS

Birmingham Town Plans

Mapseeker Archive Publishing Ltd
www.mapseeker.co.uk
www.oldmapsandimages.co.uk

Special Thanks to Birmingham Archives Services and Heritage
For the sourcing of the original 1795 and 1805 Town Plans art worked for this publication.

Pictorial Images, Views, Vistas and other Artefacts.

Mapseeker Archive Publishing Ltd
With special thanks to the following in the sourcing of antique original resources
art worked for this publication

Berian Williams Antique Maps and prints
www.antique-prints-maps.co.uk

Steve Bartrick Maps and prints
www.antiqueprints.com

Marlborough Rare books
www.marlboroughbooks.com

Jonathon Potter Antique Maps Ltd
www.jpmaps.co.uk

Lynn Hughes Artist – Mapseeker Studio
Pencil and charcoal drawing of stagecoaches passing in the night

Further Reading & Research
A History of Birmingham Places & Placenames . . . from A to Y –
http://billdargue.jimdo.com/

All of the Birmingham Town Plans and many of the pictorial plates featured in
this publication are available as photographic prints and in a range of other products on
www.mapseeker.co.uk and www.oldmapsandimages.co.uk

DEDICATION

This book is dedicated to Thomas Underwood (1809-1882) lithographer, printer, engraver and Samuel Timmins (1826-1902) Shakespearean scholar and antiquarian.

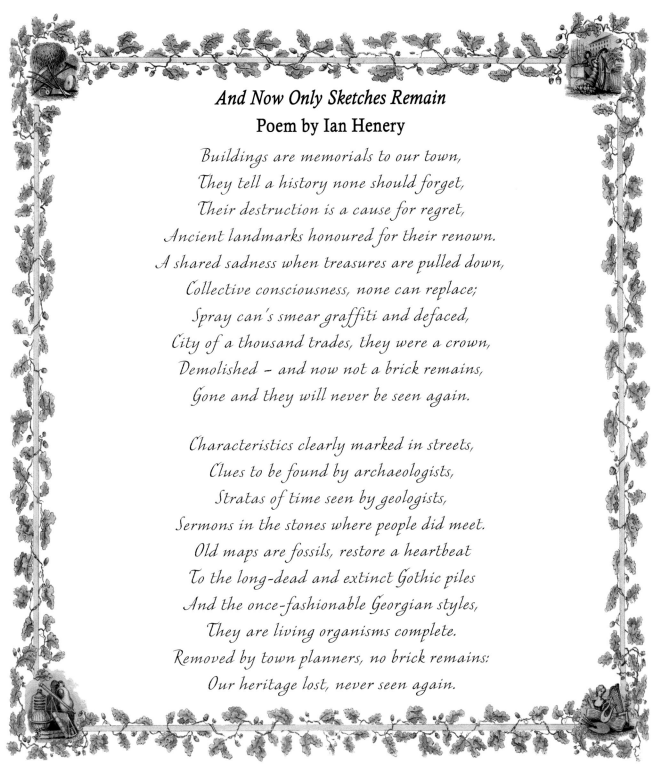

And Now Only Sketches Remain
Poem by Ian Henery

Buildings are memorials to our town,
They tell a history none should forget,
Their destruction is a cause for regret,
Ancient landmarks honoured for their renown.
A shared sadness when treasures are pulled down,
Collective consciousness, none can replace;
Spray can's smear graffiti and defaced,
City of a thousand trades, they were a crown,
Demolished – and now not a brick remains,
Gone and they will never be seen again.

Characteristics clearly marked in streets,
Clues to be found by archaeologists,
Stratas of time seen by geologists,
Sermons in the stones where people did meet.
Old maps are fossils, restore a heartbeat
To the long-dead and extinct Gothic piles
And the once-fashionable Georgian styles,
They are living organisms complete.
Removed by town planners, no brick remains:
Our heritage lost, never seen again.

RECOMMENDATIONS

Mapseeker Books – Armchair Time Travellers Series

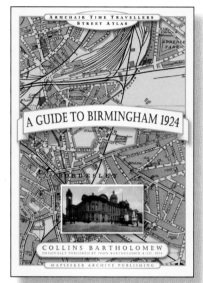

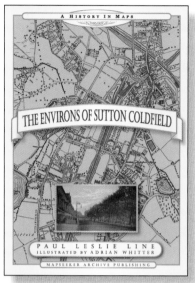

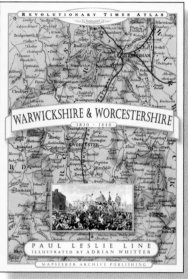

A GUIDE TO BIRMINGHAM 1924
Softcover: ISBN 9781844917433 **£19.99**

THE ENVIRONS OF SUTTON COLDFIELD
A HISTORY IN MAPS
Softcover: ISBN 9781844917808 **£19.99**

REVOLUTIONARY TIMES ATLAS OF
WARWICKSHIRE AND WORCESTERSHIRE
1830–1840
Softcover: ISBN 9781844917457 **£19.99**

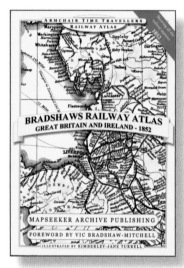

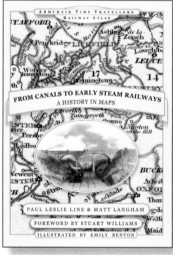

BRADSHAW'S RAILWAY ATLAS OF
GREAT BRITAIN AND IRELAND
Hardcover: ISBN 9781844917914 **£29.99**
Softcover: ISBN 9781844917907 **£19.99**

FROM CANALS TO EARLY STEAM RAILWAYS –
A HISTORY IN MAPS
Hardcover: ISBN 9781844917990 **£29.99**
Softcover: ISBN 9781844917983 **£19.99**

Birmingham Historic Maps Collection

MINING & MANUFACTURING DISTRICTS 1836 – STAFFORDSHIRE & WORCESTERSHIRE:
ISBN 9781844918188 **£14.99**

JOHN HANCOX'S MAP OF THE BIRMINGHAM CANAL NAVIGATIONS 1864:
ISBN 9781844918126 **£14.99**

JAMES DRAKES STREET PLAN AND INDEX OF BIRMINGHAM 1832:
ISBN 9781844918133 **£14.99**

SAMUEL BRADFORD TOWN PLAN BIRMINGHAM 1750:
ISBN 9781844918089 **£14.99**

THOMAS HANSON TOWN PLAN BIRMINGHAM 1778:
ISBN 9781844918096 **£14.99**